Physicians

MOUNTAIN DOCTOR

Some Other Books by LeGette Blythe

Non-fiction

MARSHAL NEY: A Dual Life
WILLIAM HENRY BELK: Merchant of the South
MIRACLE IN THE HILLS
JAMES W. DAVIS: North Carolina Surgeon
YES, MA'AM, MISS GEE
GIFT FROM THE HILLS
THOMAS WOLFE AND HIS FAMILY
(With Mabel Wolfe Wheaton)
HORNETS' NEST: The Story of Charlotte and Mecklenburg
County (With Charles R. Brockmann)
ECHO IN MY SOUL

Fiction

ALEXANDRIANA
BOLD GALILEAN
A TEAR FOR JUDAS
THE CROWN TREE
CALL DOWN THE STORM
HEAR ME, PILATE!

Drama

SHOUT FREEDOM!
VOICE IN THE WILDERNESS

MOUNTAIN DOCTOR

By LeGette Blythe

Photographs by Bruce Roberts

WILLIAM MORROW & COMPANY
New York, 1964

For Helen Whitmire McCall

MOUNTAIN DOCTOR

PROLOGUE

He's a big fellow a year or two past sixty, but when he peers at you over steel-rimmed specs his grin is boyish. His plaid sports shirt, flaring wide at his short neck, is tight about a middle usually rounded in spite of on-and-off dieting; his dark wool pants balloon unpressed at the knees. And never for long does his thick iron-graying hair betray the momentary discipline of a brush.

His name is Gaine Cannon. He is a country doctor. Over several hundred square miles of North Carolina's remotest and most inaccessible Blue Ridge Mountain coves and hills spreading out from the tiny Balsam Grove settlement, some twenty-five miles southwest of Asheville and an equal distance southeast of the Great Smoky Mountains National Park, the name Doc Cannon is magic. To many of his patients who live in cabins hidden in isolated coves and on steep mountainsides, his presence is as curative as the medicines he dispenses. In this vast region he serves, Gaine Cannon is one of the last of that fast diminishing professional group whose sturdy members have contributed immeasurably to the building and sustaining of the nation, the family doctors.

He has studied in several leading medical schools and trained in large hospitals in various sections of the nation and served a long enlistment in the United States Army's medical section, but Gaine Cannon proudly describes himself as a plain mountain doctor, available with or without pay seven days a week and twenty-four hours a day to his beloved mountain folk.

And the people of the Blue Ridge country indeed are his folk. He was born of mountain parents and claims mountain forebears generations back. His birthplace is within fifteen miles of the little hospital that—after years of community effort—he is opening to replace the clinic that he has been conducting in a remodeled farmhouse for the past decade.

Gaine Cannon is possessed by two loves. The first is the mountain folk he lives among and serves and champions. The other is Albert Schweitzer. He venerates the famous European. For him he has named his hospital the Albert Schweitzer Memorial. He has worked with the great doctor in the sprawling hospital at Lambaréné, in Equatorial Africa. Without hesitation he will declare that in his opinion Dr. Schweitzer is the greatest man, save Jesus Christ, in all the world's history. And Albert Schweitzer's philosophy of reverence for life has become, in the three decades since first he became interested in Schweitzer, his own way of life.

The passion that drives Gaine Cannon day and night, oftentimes in his little Renault or his Jeep station wagon through deep snow and bitter cold to desolate mountain shacks, is to translate into practical service to these stalwart though often poor people of his native hills the Schweitzer philosophy that the famous doctor himself has been putting to work through long years at Lambaréné.

Doc Cannon is little known outside his mountains. Trained

in general medicine, he is not a specialist in any medical field. And in no sense does he claim to be a sophisticate. But he is the great man of his region. His instinctive feel for illness and its alleviation, his generosity never measured or recorded, the strength and skill and gentleness of his sensitive, probing strong fingers, the depth of his dedication to the loving service of people of every status, his reverence for all things living, have earned him his position.

Why is he content with life deep in the hills? What forces shaped him, what motivations drive him? How has his philosophy sustained him?

This is the story of Doc Cannon and of those delightful Balsam Grove characters inextricably interwoven with him into its telling.

CHAPTER

I

"Calling Dr. Cannon. Calling Albert Schweitzer Hospital. Calling Dr. Cannon." The voice coming from the little box on the wall was insistent. "Calling the hospital. Calling Dr. Cannon."

A young man just entering from outdoors lifted the receiver. "Miz Whitmire, this here's Hugh. Doc, he's in his office with a patient. You want me to get him? . . . Yes'm . . . Yes'm . . . Aw right'm. Wait a minute, Miz Whitmire . . . Yes'm, just hold on one minute. Oh, here's Doc . . . No'm . . . Aw right, I'll tell him . . . Yes'm, just a minute."

He turned to face the big white-coated man standing in the doorway opening from an inner office into the waiting room. "Doc, Miz Whitmire says tell you one o' old man Coley's boys is over't her house. Come to get her to call you. Told her he caught a ride on a pulpwood truck after he walked down to the road. Said his old man's in bad shape and 's acallin' for you, and she's awantin' to know what to tell him."

"Did he say what was wrong with old man Coley?" The man in the doorway was squinting over the top of his old-fashioned steel-rimmed glasses. "Ask her."

The young man turned back to speak into the mouthpiece, in a moment faced the doctor again. "Said his boy said he thought his old man had a heart attack. Said he was pretty bad. He's awantin' you to get there quick as you can."

"Tell her we'll be leaving in five minutes. We'll pick him up at the filling station." The younger man relayed the message. "We may need him to help us push," the doctor added, grinning. But in the next instant he was shedding his white coat and the grin had vanished. He turned to the young woman checking through some papers at the desk near the inner door. "Helen, I reckon you'd better go up there with me and we'd better be getting started. Hugh, put the medicine case in the Jeep station wagon, and throw a mattress in the back, and some blankets. And put the oxygen tank in, too. We may have to bring him out and get him over to the hospital in Brevard. With all this snow, maybe the wagon's the only thing we can get up to his house in. And hurry, Hugh. While you're doing that, I'll run over to the apartment and get ready." He peered through the window. "I'd better wear those insulated boots and my heavy coat. Likely to need 'em."

A few minutes later, the station wagon loaded with medicines and emergency equipment, Edward Gaine Cannon, M.D., and Mrs. Helen Whitmire McCall, his laboratory technician, nurse, occasional cook and hostess, and favorite first cousin, backed away from the parking area in front of the little farmhouse converted into a clinic and headed down the lane that led to the highway. In a few moments they were clattering across the wooden bridge over Shoal Creek, which flowed in front of the farmhouse-clinic, and made a half-circle turn to come out behind it, and were passing the nearly finished stone-veneer building that would shortly, he hoped, be the functioning Albert Schweitzer Memorial Hospital. He motioned with his head toward the unfinished structure. "Helen, we surely need it, especially during this weather. It'd save a lot of hard going getting 'em over to Brevard through this kind of stuff." He grinned. "But we can get it opened maybe in another couple of years, eh?" They turned on to the highway. "We'll make it to old man Coley's and back out O.K. We've made it on many a day and night worse than this."

"The only problem will be getting from the highway up to his house," Helen observed.

"And getting back out, if it starts snowing again while we're in there," he added.

They made it. But it was after nightfall when they drove back along the lane into the little cove at Balsam Grove, to find the waiting room of the clinic filled with patients, and it was near midnight before they finished treating the last one. "It's been a pretty tough day, Helen," he said as she was putting on her coat to drive the dozen miles home. "But you know"—with his big palm he was rubbing out the creases in his forehead, and a quick smile erased the tired look—"I do believe old man Coley's going to make it. It's a good thing we got there when we did with that oxygen." He hunched his shoulders and twisted them forward and backward. "I'll try to get back out to his house sometime tomorrow"—he grinned despite his fatigue, and behind his glasses his warm eyes danced—"if the snow by then isn't neck-deep."

When she went out, he stood for a moment rubbing his hands together beside the stove in the waiting room, which before he had enclosed it had been the front porch. He had taken off the white coat that he wore in his treatment rooms and in the little obstetrics building nearby, and he stood there, relaxing after the long, hard day, in rumpled dark woolen

[14]

trousers and flannel sports shirt, in plaid pattern of white, red, and black, and open at the collar to reveal his white T shirt fitting snugly his barreling chest to the base of his short, thick neck. Standing there, now with his back to the stove but still rubbing together his agile, competent big hands, Gaine Cannon studied the framed pages of a handwritten letter from Albert Schweitzer on the wall opposite. This letter, received at Balsam Grove five years before he first met the famous European, had been written to thank him for naming his projected little institution in the Blue Ridge Mountains the Albert Schweitzer Memorial Hospital and expressing the hope that someday the two physicians might meet. "Reverence for life," Dr. Cannon said solemnly, as if to the framed letter itself, "reverence for life. He's a great man, Hugh"—he turned to face Hugh Purvis, his man-of-all-work, companion and friend, and once again his smile seemed to drive away the fatigue—"the greatest." Then suddenly his mood changed. "Hugh, let's go over to the apartment and have something to eat, a bowl of soup and crackers and a salad. Maybe a steak. Reckon you could eat a steak? Come to think of it, I haven't had a bite since early this morning." He stepped to the window to pull the curtains apart and peer up the snow-covered lane. "There won't be any more patients coming tonight."

"Doc, I sure hope not." Hugh was fervent.

"I hope not too," Gaine Cannon agreed. "I'd like to get a little sleep between now and morning." His forehead creased again, and little crow's-feet tracked outward from the corners of his eyes. "I wonder how old man Coley's doing."

CHAPTER

2

PERHAPS three fourths of Gaine Cannon's routine twenty-four-hour day is spent in his clinic beside the creek, in the mountain homes of patients within a three-county region centering about Balsam Grove, and in the little red Renault in which customarily he makes his calls.

But when any time, day or night, his waiting room is momentarily cleared of patients and no calls for him have come in over his two-way radio, the only voice communication he has with the outside world, or on his return from a call no one is waiting with a message summoning him to visit an ailing or injured person back in the hills, he will slip over to his apartment for something to eat and a hurried nap. Sometimes, though rarely, he is able to sleep four to six hours undisturbed. Sometimes, too, though infrequently, he may enjoy a leisurely meal. More often, however, he has a bowl of soup, poured from a can and hurriedly heated, and crackers, with beets or cucumber pickles or sauerkraut or sliced tomatoes or pickled snap beans, some from cans, some from glass jars sent him by patients, with a cup of instant coffee or a glass of milk.

Usually he eats while standing before the drainboard of his kitchen sink; sometimes he clears away a little space on his cluttered desk a few feet away in the living room and sits down to eat there.

At arm's length from the gas stove in the tiny kitchen is his open-shelved pantry, and always it is stocked to running over with canned meats and vegetables, fruits, preserves, cereals, jellies, syrup, cake mixes, meal, flour, sugar, and staples of every kind.

"I'm always afraid that we might get really snowed in sometime, and I want to have plenty of food on hand in case of an emergency," he says. "And I like to have enough to be able to take some out to a needy family without having to go to a grocery store. But in spite of having so much food around all the time—and my patients are always giving me things, too—I often go for a whole day without stopping to eat, particularly if I'm here at the clinic. If you are in a patient's home at mealtime, though, you just have to eat with him. But still I don't seem to be able to reduce consistently. I even eat this low-calorie food and go for days with little more than these new diet drinks. But then when I'm down maybe twenty pounds and half starved (and I should lose more) I go on an eating binge and consume enough for a horse." He shakes his head glumly. "I'm not very good at following my own prescriptions for myself."

Paradoxically, it was a physician's advice which sent Gaine Cannon to Balsam Grove; and then it was Cannon's disregard of that advice which started his practice here. Eleven years ago a doctor friend ordered him to take a long rest. That was when Gaine Cannon was practicing in Pickens, South Carolina, a small town twenty miles below the states' boundary line. For years his practice had kept him going day and night.

"Gaine, you're killing your fool self," this doctor had told him bluntly. "If you don't stop and take it easy for a while, you're going to die. You may die pretty soon anyway, but I'm absolutely sure you will if you don't take a long rest."

For some time Dr. Cannon had suffered with a back ailment that had persisted after an operation for a ruptured spinal disc followed by a long period of hospitalization. He had experienced some heart difficulty, too, and the strain of heavy practice was not improving that situation.

So he promised his doctor and himself that he would obey his friend's emphatic orders. He would take off several weeks, maybe months, and get a thorough rest. He would leave his South Carolina practice and go off somewhere and relax completely. He would do nothing but sleep and eat, take strolls through the fields and woods, sit in his rocking chair, and rock and read. He needed to catch up on his reading. From his childhood he had enjoyed books; as a student in college and medical school he had devoted much of whatever little leisure he could find between studying and earning his way to general reading, and during his years of practice he had bought books and subscribed to national periodicals and read them whenever opportunity permitted. But he had missed many books of importance in various fields—politics, philosophy and religion, world affairs, biographies, novels, both current and among the classics—and some of these he might be able now to look into.

And very likely, Dr. Cannon told himself, even though he had bought and read every book and magazine article by or about Dr. Schweitzer that he had learned of, there were recently published ones of which he hadn't heard. Some of those he had read he would like to read a second time and more thoroughly digest. He would have opportunity to consider quietly and calmly, to meditate upon, to weigh and measure and seek to define for himself his own philosophy in relation to Albert Schweitzer's.

In the years since he had first read of Dr. Schweitzer and his reverence for all things living, Gaine Cannon's interest in the great European had grown from respect and admiration to veneration and more and more he had found that his own concepts of existence, embracing such elementals as God and nature and man and their relationships, as far as he could discover them for himself, seemed to be completely in harmony with those of Dr. Schweitzer as best he could understand the Schweitzer philosophy.

Nothing could be more pleasing to him and more rewarding, he told himself, than to go away from his heavy and exacting duties as a physician and sit down for a while to rest, read, and ruminate upon the strange mystery of life and men's varying attitudes toward it.

And fortunately, Gaine Cannon knew where to go. He had bought a farm up in his native North Carolina mountains, a place back in a cove through which a pleasant stream twisted, a small cove all but surrounded by hills and reached only by a straggling dirt road hardly traversable except in good weather. The cove was about half a mile from the Balsam Grove post office. He would go up to Balsam Grove and spend a while there in the farmhouse beside the creek.

So one day he got into his car and drove up to his farm. He brought a supply of groceries and enough furniture and bedding to serve his modest needs. He had decided without reservation to rest and rebuild his depleted physical resources; he had promised himself as well as his doctor that he would even put out of his mind his patients and the small hospital whose building and operation had kept him under a never relieved strain and tension the past several years.

He hadn't been in Balsam Grove a day and night before he

realized that he couldn't have found a more ideal spot in which to rest and recuperate. He was shut away in a cove, hidden from a highway little traveled, with no neighbors crowding him, and praise be, miles from a telephone. All his life people had been his greatest interest and concern, but at the same time, with their aches and pains and other problems, people had been the main cause of his own impaired health. Now for a time, until he chose to return to them, he would be free of people, he would forget that there were such things as pills and penicillin.

This place would be a balm and bring healing. The hills surrounding the cove on all sides except where the creek came into it, and circling, slipped out with the rough road, the high altitude even of the cove's floor, would quickly lift his spirits. The sounds would add their healing, the rhythmic murmuring of his little stream, the plaintive soughing of the wind through the white pines and the balsams, even the distant baying of hounds, and in the night the sudden shattering scream of the wildcat, the eerie call of the screech owl, and the deep guttural *who-who* of the larger brother, these would be for him soothing, remembered music. And the little sounds, too, the twitterings of small birds in the apple tree overhanging the creek, the hum of bees and the chirping of crickets, even the sudden strident staccato in August of innumerable cicadas and the throaty croakings of frogs. Here nature's harmony would lull and soothe; in the hill country he would happily be rid of the raucous discords of peopled places.

To this synthesis of nature's sounds, Gaine Cannon knew also, nature would be offering for his enjoyment and replenishment a harmony of colors—balsams and pines and rhododendron and mountain laurel in varying tints and shades of green, the browns of tree trunks and broomstraw and fallen leaves, and in the autumn the glory on the hillsides of nature's perfect intermixing of reds and yellows and greens and oranges and browns and purples, and always, on every sunny day, the subtle changing of the cove's coloring with the sweep of the sun above one mountain top at midmorning and its disappearance beyond the opposite one at midafternoon.

So on a bright morning, after he had risen late and breakfasted leisurely, Gaine Cannon picked up one of the Schweitzer volumes and went out to the porch. He moved his chair to the corner where he could see all the way on two sides of the house. He would keep his eyes and his ears open to the sights and sounds of nature's harmony, unspoiled by the tampering and trespassing of people. And all the while he would be ruminating upon the teachings of Albert Schweitzer and trying to apply to his own situation Schweitzer's principle of reverence for life.

From the porch corner he could look along the winding of Shoal Creek to the point where it disappeared through the narrow gorge between two steep hills. Immediately the practical thinking that had already guided him through the planning, building, and operating of two small community hospitals helped him envision the construction in this gap of a dam that would provide a large lake covering the meadow in the valley upstream. But at that moment it was only a dream; he could not foresee that ten years later the dream would begin to materialize with the arrival of surveyors and engineers and men riding bulldozers. Just as quickly he dismissed the thought. The building of a dam and a lake above it would take planning and work and people and machines, and commotion and carbon monoxide ruining the quiet and primeval peace of the cove, and he had come into it for physical and psychological rejuvenation.

He had come up to Balsam Grove to think and ponder, to consider nature and man and God, the attributes of each, the role of each in the grand scheme of existence. Wouldn't this be a wonderful, tremendous, perfect place in which to spend with Albert Schweitzer an hour or a day or a month or a lifetime? Here in these mountains alone with the good and great doctor wouldn't one be truly in harmony with all life, wouldn't one find fellowship not only with this great soul but with the wild animals, the birds, the trees and flowers, even the unfraternizing insects? Wouldn't Albert Schweitzer love this pleasant, isolated, unspoiled cove between the hills? Wouldn't he exult, after all those years in the steaming jungles of Equatorial Africa, in the exhilarating cool greenness of a delightful region still untrampled, still free of the clutter and confusion of people?

In that same instant Gaine Cannon knew that in thus imagining Albert Schweitzer lolling in Balsam Grove he had, if only in his imagination, betrayed the man whom, of all men on earth, he venerated most. He knew that Albert Schweitzer would enjoy immensely the climate of the mountains and their natural beauty and in the little cove would feel an affinity with all its burgeoning life. But he also knew that the great doctor would never choose to remain long in any place where there were no people to whom he could minister, no ill and injured and suffering humanity to whose comforting and curing he might offer his prayers and his capable, strong hands. Had he not spent his life in dedication to serving people, poor, frightened, sorrowing, and suffering people, little advanced from savagery, far beneath the level of the most illiterate, the most isolated, the poorest folk in all the mountains?

If by chance Albert Schweitzer had come into this cove, Gaine Cannon reasoned as he watched the water rippling over the rounded rocks, if he had come here to live or even to settle for a while, he no doubt would have built a small hospital for the treatment of the mountain folk, who most certainly would have swarmed to him as the Africans had been crowding for years into the compound at Lambaréné.

Indeed, the Balsam Grove folk should have medical service, even, perhaps, a small hospital. Gaine Cannon approved of the course he imagined the great doctor would have taken in providing one. No doctor lives within miles of the tiny post office in the center of the community, and when one comes out from Brevard he must charge twenty-five dollars or more for the visit, which in bad weather may require most of a day. And what resident of these cabins in the hills can pay such a fee for a doctor's visit?

Yet these are good people, deserving the best from life, Dr. Cannon told himself, folk, whether affluent or desperately poor, who respect their neighbors and themselves, demonstrating in their humble but positive way their respect and reverence for the life around them. Yet all about him on this bright morning, for miles out from this little cove, good mountain folk were suffering and some perhaps were dying for lack of medical help. A doctor right here could provide immeasurable service, could with far-reaching results put a philosophy into practice. A doctor here in this little cove could transform a community, could make meaningful his reverence for life. And with a small hospital properly equipped—Gaine Cannon turned from watching the creek flowing past him to look over his left shoulder—a small hospital back there in that flat just the other side of the bridge, set with its rear wall snuggled against the steep hillside and its front windows looking out upon the opposite hillside rising steeply beyond the creek . . .

Sitting there on his little porch in the cool of the morning, he built his hospital. Stone upon stone its walls arose—angular, rough granite from the steep hillsides and rounded, smooth rocks from the mountain streams—and partitions divided and rooms appeared—wards, private rooms, an operating room, an obstetrics wing where mountain mothers could have their babies safely and with a minimum of pain—and beds and dressers and other needed equipment and furnishings. And he saw doctors—surgeons, an obstetrician, an internist—and nurses—dedicated and trained mountain girls serving their people. But more clearly he envisioned the patients gathered in from the coves and the ridges, men and women and children, bearded patriarchs and newborn infants—comfortably fixed, desperately poor, good, bad, indifferent, but people in need, in pain, in despair, people who required him, *his* people.

Gaine Cannon knew in that moment, as surely as he had ever known any truth, that the thinking and the example of Albert Schweitzer, *his* greatest man on earth, applied to his own reasoning and hoping, envisioned and demanded the realizing of the institution he was seeing so realistically. How else could he so effectively live and demonstrate the soundness, the rightness, of Albert Schweitzer's philosophy, of *his* philosophy, than to minister in the most dedicated way, the most effective manner, to these people of his mountains, *his* people? How else?

But quickly now he turned from the temptation of his conjuring to watch a covey of quail venturing from behind the other building in the cove, a crude structure that had given scant protection to the previous owner's battered pickup. Hadn't he promised his doctor to forget doctoring and hospitals for a while? Hadn't he left South Carolina to get away from his hospital, from his patients? And up here in Balsam Grove hadn't he found the one place where he could do that?

CHAPTER

3

As Gaine Cannon sat on the front porch of his little farm-house in the bend of softly purling, pebbled Shoal Creek, he was a mountaineer come home. Fifty-five years before he had been born a dozen miles northeastward, across the ridge in the little settlement of Calvert, north of the French Broad River, a mile beyond Rosman, a village nine miles southwest of Brevard, North Carolina, on U S Highway 64. Brevard, county seat of Transylvania County, is about twenty-five miles southwest of Asheville. It is that far as a plane would fly over the Blue Ridge Parkway, and some of the most rugged terrain in eastern America; measured along the twists of the river it is twice or three times that far.

Dr. Cannon has always been proud of being a mountaineer. His mother was a Whitmire from this same Transylvania County in North Carolina. The Whitmires are a long-estab-lished family in this section, and a little south of Rosman there are still quite a number of them, although in the immediate vicinity of Balsam Grove virtually everybody is a McCall or an Owen or a Galloway, everybody except two or three

[25]

Kitchens and one family of Masons. A few years ago, before North Carolina's school consolidation program was extended to embrace even the more isolated and less populous mountain communities, they had a school in Balsam Grove in which every pupil on the roll, with the exception of two, was either a McCall or an Owen. Through his mother Gaine Cannon is related to many of these members of the older Transylvania families.

His father was a doctor. His father, too, was almost mountain-born. He was a Georgian, a native of Rabun County, which sits at the foot of the mountains and adjoins both North Carolina and South Carolina in the extreme northeastern corner of Georgia. Young Dr. James Alvin Cannon had hardly finished his medical training when he crossed over into North Carolina and came up into Transylvania County. "He got bored with living at home and just walked off," Gaine Cannon explains. "I remember hearing his older sisters and brothers, my aunts and uncles, telling us how Father left home and they didn't know where he was until an older brother and sister came upon him up here in this neighborhood. Evidently he had given little thought to beginning his career as a doctor. When they found him, he wasn't practicing; he was playing croquet.

"But at that time Father was only a boy. Back in those days a young man who wanted to become a physician only had to have a certificate from a schoolteacher recommending him for acceptance to get into a medical school. And after he was admitted, he had but two years of medicine, with only five months of study each year. Upon completion of that training, the incipient doctor 'read medicine,' as it was termed then, with some practicing physician; after that he was considered competent to begin his practice. Father had taken his two years of training at what is now Emory University, in

Atlanta; it was then called, I believe, the Southern Medical College."

Though the young Dr. James Cannon must have been reluctant to undertake at that time the grueling responsibilities of the country physician, he was prevailed upon by his brother and sister to return with them to Georgia, where he soon established a practice.

"Not for long, however," Gaine Cannon says. "The mountains were calling him, or maybe he had met the young Miss Whitmire who would be our mother. At any rate, he closed his office in Georgia and came back up here and established his practice, and pretty soon he married. When I was three or four years old—I can just remember it—the family moved southward some thirty miles to Pickens, South Carolina. But Father continued to practice over a wide area up here in the North Carolina mountains, and after he got to be an old man he would come up to Rosman every now and then and open a little office, from which he would ride the roads and twisting trails to attend patients in Jackson and Transylvania counties.

"In those days, particularly during his early practice, Father had to do most of his traveling on horseback, carrying his medicines and his instruments in his saddlebags. He rode long distances, and not only were the calls tiring and time-consuming, but he was also often paid poorly. Father could hardly make a call far over into Jackson County and get back the same day. And often he collected not a penny. I still wonder how he ever made a living. Few of his patients had much money, and many had hardly any. And sometimes those who were able to pay him wouldn't do it, even though he charged little. I have wondered about his fees, too; I think he must have charged about what he thought he could get, which must never have been much. Most of the time he was paid in things the family could eat—a country ham, potatoes, fresh vegetables, apples, cabbage, canned berries, fruits, and vegetables, strawberry and blackberry preserves, jams, honey, molasses, string beans, and kraut, produce like that from the farms and orchards. Father couldn't carry much of that sort of stuff on his horse, along with his bulging saddlebags, so often a patient would bring it down to us, sometimes in a cart pulled by an ox."

Oftentimes, in fact, that is the only pay Gaine Cannon himself gets, things to eat. Usually the shelves of the pantry in his apartment are crammed with canned fruits and vegetables, and boxes on the floor are loaded with potatoes, cabbage, turnips, and turnip greens. "Some patients have paid me by coming in to do work on the hospital construction; many have brought smooth river stones and sand with which we have been veneering the concrete block walls of the structure. When they pay me that way, I give them half their wages in cash and the other half is credited to their hospital and doctor bills. That gives them some money and at the same time helps us along toward the day when we'll have our hospital and community project well on the way to full realization." More than forty thousand hours of labor have already been contributed, Dr. Cannon estimates.

But fruits and vegetables, fresh or canned, fresh meat and cured, milk, eggs and butter, and the like, and hours of labor on the hospital building and about the grounds are not the only contributions Dr. Cannon receives as gifts or in payment of fees for his professional services.

"One day I received word to go out to the house of a confirmed alcoholic. He was in a bad way, and I gave him glucose and worked with him for quite a time. But he came around all right and was up and about before I left him.

"Two days later I was making a call at a mountain home. I

[28]

had stopped and was reaching in the back of the car for my bag when I felt something hard and round. Investigating, I found three gallons of corn whiskey. My alcoholic patient had managed to slip the whiskey into the car and I had been hauling the stuff around all that time without knowing it."

But Dr. Cannon considers the most unusual payment he has ever received that given him by a young redheaded mountain man who came over to the obstetrics clinic at Balsam Grove late one afternoon.

"Doc, my wife is afixin' to have a baby," he revealed, "an' I come over here to see if you'll take care of her." He grinned sheepishly. "I already owe you for one baby."

"Why'd you tell me that?" the doctor asked him. "I didn't remember it; I would never have thought about it if you hadn't told me."

"Well, Doc, I want to pay my debts. I ain't in no notion o' gettin' out o' payin'. And if you'll look after her, Doc, I've got a couple o' television sets that I'll fetch over here and let you keep 'em till I can pay the bill."

"Well, I never asked you for the money, did I?"

"No, you didn't, Doc," he replied. "But I aim to pay you. An' I'm agoin' to fetch them televisions over here."

So he brought two battered second-hand sets, worth perhaps, the two of them, thirty or forty dollars, and neither in operating condition.

Dr. Cannon took care of his wife at the clinic; she had her baby very quickly after she arrived, for many mountain couples never think of seeing the doctor until the wife has begun to have labor pains. The husband came for her. He was walking. So Dr. Cannon had one of his nurses drive them home, after he had given them medicine, including worm treatments for their other children. They thanked him

[29]

warmly. And when they arrived home, they thanked the nurse for bringing them and helping with the delivery. "I tell you what I'm agoin' to do," the man said to her. "T'other day I took in another television on a trade, and I fixed it. This here one works, and I'm agoin' to give it to Doc Cannon, and I want you to take it back to him." She did. It worked for a while.

Dr. Cannon wondered how this man happened to be repairing television sets. It is an unlikely occupation for a fellow living in a two-room cabin at the end of a straggly road in the backside of an isolated cove in an area that does not have many television sets. The house had one fairly large room that served as living room, dining room, and kitchen, but the other room was very small. Yet the couple had five or six children, and the man's mother, an elderly woman, lived with them. So the two rooms were crowded, yet in that little house he also did his television repairing.

The house had no electricity. The doctor reasoned that the man had some sort of battery-powered apparatus with which he tested the television sets. More amazing, he had sent off somewhere for a correspondence course in television repair although he could not read, and when he received the instructional material he had to get someone to read it to him.

Once this man had gone over to Hendersonville, some forty miles from his home, to work in a television repair shop, Dr. Cannon learned, but he had not been happy until he returned to his own mountain community. Since his return he had been going through the country selling sets that he bought for ten or fifteen dollars and repaired; he got these sets from stores and repair shops to which they had been turned in as trades on new sets, and after repairing them he sold them to his mountain neighbors. But of course his business was slow, and it was difficult for him to make a living from it for himself and his family. Lately the man has had his shop in a small store, but it is also about as isolated as such a place could be.

"So it has been a precarious existence for that family," Gaine Cannon says. "And with a new baby coming every year, the problem of making a living has become progressively more difficult. I have delivered two or three of their children; I remember that one baby died when he was still very young; he was smothered to death sleeping between his parents. Now and then in the mountains one hears of a baby's being smothered that way. Bedding is at a premium oftentimes, and children pile in bed with their fathers and mothers; sometimes a parent will turn over in the night and inadvertently smother an infant. I think that's what happened in this case."

One winter when there was an unusually heavy snow in the Transylvania County area, Gaine Cannon went out with one of the young women on his staff to take some provisions to the television man's family. He was afraid they were cut off and perhaps suffering; even in good weather it was always touch-and-go whether that family would have enough to eat. The doctor had put four snow tires on his Jeep station wagon and chains on the snow tires, and even then he and his nurse had trouble pushing their way back into the cove. The snow was at least a foot deep over the level places and on the road, which was hardly more than a trail in good weather, and this climbing, twisting trail was difficult to follow. Much of the way the doctor had to race his vehicle forward ten or fifteen feet to break his way through the snow. Then he would be stalled and have to back up in order to make a new start; he'd run forward in the tracks he had just beaten out until he stalled again. But finally they made it to the fellow's cabin.

[31]

They took the groceries inside, and there they discovered the family, with the old lady, huddled over a puny fire.

"We were afraid you couldn't get out to get anything to eat," Gaine Cannon told them. "The snow's mighty deep, and a lot of folks are snowbound. So we thought we'd bring you some groceries to tide you over awhile."

Mountain folk, rich or poor, are proud. Dr. Cannon did not want to offend them by implying that he considered them charity cases.

They were happy to get the food, and it was evident by the way they fell upon it that they were famished. They might actually have starved in another few days if Dr. Cannon hadn't been able to get to them. About a month later the doctor made another trip into their remote cove to bring them another supply of food. "I hope you won't be embarrassed if we bring you some more groceries," Dr. Cannon said when the television man greeted him at his door.

"No, sir, Doc," the grateful fellow assured him. "It's just like having another Christmas to get them groceries."

"Seeing those folk enjoy that food, and particularly the children, and the looks in the young parents' eyes," Dr. Cannon says "was pay enough, and more, for the expense and effort of taking those groceries out there. I suspect that's one kind of payment a doctor gets"—there's a gleam in his eyes as he says it—"that a fellow who isn't a doctor just doesn't know about, particularly if he isn't a doctor back in the mountains."

CHAPTER

4

GAINE CANNON cannot remember when first he decided to become a doctor. One of the first things he can recall about those days sixty years ago when his father moved the family to Pickens was his playing doctor. "I would always be the doctor and some other child would be the patient," he remembers. "It never occurred to me to be the patient and let the other youngster be the doctor. And the neighbors even back then used to say that I would grow up to be a doctor, my older brother a lawyer, and my younger brother, who was born about the time we moved to South Carolina, a preacher. It didn't work out that way, except for me. My older brother, Ruhl, named for a Revolutionary soldier, came nearer to being a doctor than a lawyer. He became a successful pharmacist; he died five years ago. My younger brother, Glenn Alvin Cannon, did not become a preacher, but I would describe him as a philosopher as well as an artist. He lives in Columbia, South Carolina. In his painting, however, he has shown a theological bent; he is soon to bring out a book of paintings on Old Testament subjects.

"Father combined my profession and Ruhl's. Like me, he had to be both doctor and pharmacist. He must have compounded most of his medicines, although in his day few kinds were prescribed. Calomel was generally given, and CCC pills. I can recall as a youngster taking calomel how drastic that treatment was. Calomel had about as much gentleness of action as a stick of dynamite. Maybe my remembering how it affected me, how deathly sick I felt after swallowing a dose of the stuff, has had something to do with the fact that I have never in all my life prescribed one dose of calomel. Few doctors have, I suspect, in the last thirty or forty years.

"When I was a child, people used to be afraid that in taking calomel they might become what they called 'salivated.' You never hear that word any more. I have seen a few cases of salivation, and they are frightening. The term comes from the salivary glands, which secrete saliva, and it used to denote the effects of calomel on the calcium in the body. Often in especially severe cases—and I have heard my father tell of such cases that he had been called to treat—the teeth would become loose and fall out and sometimes the patient would lose his hair. Fortunately, you never hear of calomel's causing anybody to be salivated nowadays; in fact, you rarely hear of calomel any more."

When Gaine Cannon was a very small youngster, he went with his father on calls about the countryside, riding behind him on horseback or sitting beside him in the doctor's buggy. But Dr. Cannon did not want the boy to be a doctor. In fact, Gaine Cannon remembers very distinctly his father was quite determined that his son would not study medicine. He insisted that the life of the physician, and particularly of a general practitioner in a rural community, was too hard.

"It's rough, Son," he would declare. "A doctor is riding day and night in all kinds of weather. He never gets enough sleep and never gets much money. You get into something else, boy."

The elder Cannon lectured his son on the hard life of a doctor even as the youngster was riding behind him astride the horse and sometimes in a storm that overtook them returning from a call; he continued to remonstrate years later when Gaine, then thirteen or fourteen, was driving him on calls in the automobile the doctor would never learn to drive.

"But I refused to heed his insistent advice," Dr. Cannon reveals. "I was still determined to study medicine, and I told him so. And as I grew older, I didn't seem to be able to get along with him. The years from fourteen to eighteen, when I should have been doing my high school work, I was continually running away from home. I worked at many jobs; I earned my living while I was away, but it was tough. I worked in cotton mills, at tanneries, at sawmills. Once I ran away and was gone three months. When my sister Ruth, who by then was married, succeeded in finding me, I was working in a South Carolina cotton mill, making a dollar a day. Ruth took me home, and Father promptly gave me a sound thrashing. He would do that now and then, even after I was well into the teens, and I resented it. I felt, too, that he was partial to my older brother, and that this was responsible for some of the punishment I had been getting. This resentment, I suspect, made me all the more determined to be a doctor. Certainly it was responsible for my deciding to go back to school, because I realized that if I was to be a doctor I would have to have the required training. So at eighteen, when I should have graduated from high school, I stopped running away from home and began to study hard. In two and a half years I was able to earn my high school diploma. I knew then that I was going to study medicine, that nothing would cause me to change my mind. But I knew also that I would have to complete the preliminary college work. And the more Father opposed my plans, the more determined I became."

One day, a week or so after he had finished high school, young Cannon announced to his mother that he was going off to college. He was planning to leave within the next few days, he said. "I'm going to be a doctor," he declared, "and I'm going to college right away and get started on it. I'm going to Berea College, out in Kentucky."

"But, Son," his mother protested, "college won't be open now. It won't be starting again until September. How'll you manage until then? And how'll you manage during the regular term?" They were sensible questions, young Cannon knew, for his father would never be able to send him to college on the money earned by a country doctor even if he had been eager to do so. But young Cannon was confident that he himself could manage.

"I'll get a job and I'll get along," he assured his mother. "You all won't have to worry about me, and you won't have to send me any money, either."

So Gaine Cannon packed a few belongings in a battered suitcase and went out to Kentucky. Berea College was then, as it has continued to be, an institution where the student could work his way through. And though it was more than two months until the fall term would start, the college authorities allowed him to enroll and gave him a job. It was not a very good-paying job, but he managed to get along, as he had assured his mother he would. Soon he had a better-paying job, this one in the college hospital, and one of his duties was to drive the ambulance. He continued to drive the ambulance, in fact, as long as he was at Berea, and the assignment proved to be good experience. For three of his years at Berea he also worked in the operating room as assistant to a surgeon, and the experience there was of even more value. When finally he was able to enroll in medical school, he discovered that he knew much about surgery that the other beginning students did not. But he also knew better than to say anything to his professors about it.

Gaine Cannon received his Bachelor's degree from Berea College at the 1925 commencement. He planned to enter medical school in the fall and had made tentative arrangements to study at the University of Edinburgh. His plans for the summer months were novel and interesting. In the spring of his senior year at Berea he had been impressed by the performance of a troupe of gymnasts from the Gymnastik Höjskole, operated in Ollerup, Denmark, by the then famous Niels Buck.

After watching these well-muscled and graceful athletes perform, Gaine Cannon decided he would go to Ollerup and enroll for a summer course. He was tired and in poor physical shape to begin an arduous four years of studying medicine, he felt, and a summer in physical training should be of great value to him.

When he boarded the train at Berea after his graduation, he had twelve dollars. But he had considerable confidence and determination. He would figure out some scheme for financing his summer. His medical course had been provided for; one of his high school teachers, a woman, had agreed to lend him enough money, to be added to what he himself could earn, to see him through Edinburgh.

He took his seat on the train, his college work behind him, and began to devise some way of paying his passage to Europe. Always, he knew, there were the cattle boats.

And then, only minutes before the train was to leave, he saw through the window a group of his friends piling out of the ambulance he had driven. They swarmed over to the train —the surgeon he had worked with, nurses at the infirmary, school friends. They handed him a going-away present. When he opened it, he discovered it was a purse of more than two hundred dollars.

But he didn't spend the money for steamship passage. Instead he worked his way across the Atlantic on a cattle boat from Montreal to Glasgow.

At Ollerup he entered the Gymnastik Höjskole, and there he worked hard to build himself up physically. When late in the summer he went to Glasgow to enroll in the medical school, he was fit and in an excellent mood to begin the grueling work.

But there he was to get the staggering news that the woman who had agreed to advance him the required funds had suffered financial reverses; she had no money to lend him, and he could make no arrangements with the institution for paying his way. So he decided, since it was too late to make further plans with any other medical school for the coming session, to return to Ollerup and continue his training in physical education. And when he returned to the United States the following summer, he considered himself in perfect health.

It was fortunate that he was, for soon he would be entering a period of hard study and work that after almost forty years has been interrupted only during the infrequent times he has been hospitalized. During the time he took his training in medicine, he studied at the Medical College of Virginia at Richmond, the universities of Kentucky, Wisconsin, and Michigan, and Western Reserve University, in Cleveland. He finally earned his Doctor of Medicine degree at the Medical College of Virginia.

"My going to all those medical schools might seen to indicate that I flunked out of one after another," he observes. "But actually I didn't. I was taking my basic work at the Medical College of Virginia, but all the time I was at Richmond I had to earn my way, and I was working as an assistant in anatomy. I made quite a bit of money that way, but having that assistantship prevented my taking the full course during the nine-month regular terms. My duty was to work each year with the first-year medical students, instructing them in dissecting bodies. I liked that work, too; the study of anatomy was very interesting to me, so interesting, in fact, that I planned to go into surgery. But I began to have trouble with my back and I couldn't stand long hours, which would have been necessary if I had been a surgeon. When years later I discovered that I had a ruptured disc, it was too late.

"But because I was an assistant in anatomy all this time and could not take the full medical course during the regular terms, I enrolled for summer-session short courses in other medical schools, and in that way I kept up with my classes at the Medical College of Virginia."

Gaine Cannon received his Doctor of Medicine degree in June 1931. From Richmond he went to St. Elizabeth's Lying-In and Children's Hospital, a government hospital in Washington, for a two-year rotating internship. In that period of further training he gained experience in obstetrics and pediatrics that in later practice, particularly during his years in the North Carolina mountains, would be invaluable.

When his internship was completed in 1933, the country was in the depths of the depression. Some of his classmates who had gone into private practice after a year of interning had not made enough money to keep up the installment payments on their office furniture and equipment. But Dr. Cannon had a commission in the Army Reserve, so he went into the Civilian Conservation Corps, which in that depression period provided jobs and a living for a host of unemployed youths. "That gave me enough money for me to pay off some debts, at least," he says. And he is always quick to defend that organization's record. "Some critics insist the CCC was a waste of money. Perhaps money was wasted in some instances, as is always the case when large sums are spent in emergency programs. But the CCC did more than put out Roosevelt pine trees. It did many other things that have been of considerable value to the nation. But more important, it gave jobs and a decent living to many young men who without its help might have lost their way."

The camp to which Dr. Cannon was assigned was near Ridgway in northwestern Pennsylvania. Three small villages in that vicinity had no doctor, he soon discovered, and the government, at the urging of citizens, gave him permission to treat them; Pennsylvania granted him a temporary license. The work was hard and wearing. Often it was late at night when he went to bed. One night, utterly weary, he went to sleep while driving. When he was aroused by a sudden terrific impact, he found himself off the road, among a pile of boulders. He had shattered all four wheels, burst his tires, and damaged his fenders. The accident cost him more than three hundred dollars.

While Dr. Cannon was stationed at the CCC camp in Pennsylvania he learned from a Pickens friend, Dr. R. A. Allgood, who had been practicing fifteen or twenty years at Fayetteville, North Carolina, where Fort Bragg, the nation's largest military encampment, is located, of a position available in a village on the outskirts of Fayetteville. Dr. Allgood arranged for the job to be offered to Dr. Cannon. He was to serve as physician in the village under the sponsorship of a large textile mill operating there.

Gaine Cannon accepted the offer and went down and set up an office. This small place had no pharmacist, and the doctor had to fill his own prescriptions. Nor was there running water; he used a hand pump. His work was demanding, and the hours were long. But he interrupted his practice long enough in 1936 to go back to Pennsylvania to get married. He had found one young woman at Ridgway particularly attractive, and they had corresponded when he returned to North Carolina to establish his practice. After their marriage and wedding trip they began housekeeping, and within a year he built a clinic that has since expanded into a small hospital. That was his first venture in developing medical facilities, and it was a heavy assignment added to his already burdensome work. But it was a challenge, too, and stimulating, and he would learn much of practical value from the experience.

The Cannons remained there about five years, and all the while the doctor's duties grew more onerous. The task of attending to the medical needs of that community virtually without help had drained his physical resources, and he was almost exhausted. His weight dropped from a normal of about 185 pounds to 133.

"I was going day and night. I just couldn't get enough sleep. I remember many a time I'd stop at a creek and wash my face to try to keep awake. Sometimes I'd get so sleepy I'd actually be sick. And even then I'd often get home from a very late call and find two or three patients waiting for me. It was discouraging."

The international situation, too, was discouraging; it appeared that war was imminent. Dr. Cannon had maintained his membership in the Army Reserve and was glad he had. He decided to return to active duty, and in 1940 volunteered for service.

CHAPTER

5

His new duties didn't take Dr. Cannon far from the village in which he had been practicing. He was assigned, with the rank of captain, to nearby Fort Bragg, then rapidly filling with soldiers. "There wasn't much difference in my practice," he recalls. "I was made post surgeon, which meant that I had the responsibility of caring for the families of both the commissioned and noncommissioned officers at the fort. And it meant, too, that I would be getting no more rest in my new job than I had been getting the last five years in my general practice, maybe less. But it was an interesting assignment because I got to know in a very close and personal way many famous men in the service and their families. From time to time I treated General Mark Clark and members of his family; General George Patton, the famous 'Old Blood and Guts,' and his wife; General Devers; General Patch; and others whose names were almost daily in the headlines. General Patch died of pneumonia in Texas not long after I had treated him at Fort Bragg. Clark at that time was a colonel. I was in Patton's home many times to see his wife, who was sick much of the time they were at Bragg. Patton was always cracking jokes, usually at the expense of 'you medics,' as he called the doctors. He always carried two pistols; he was quite a character. I particularly liked the Clarks; Mrs. Clark was especially pleasant and considerate. They had two or three children, and I was called to their home quite often. For a long time now I have been trying to get down to Charleston, South Carolina, where General Clark is the president of The Citadel, to talk over old times with them."

But Dr. Cannon's assignment at Fort Bragg was interrupted. His back began to give him trouble again, and he was sent to Starke General Hospital, at Charleston, South Carolina, where an operation was performed and he was placed in a rigid cast that virtually immobilized him for five months. He remained in the hospital three months after the cast was removed. The confinement aggravated his claustrophobia; even now he looks back upon those days in the cast with abhorrence.

After his return to Fort Bragg he was transferred to the Women's Army Corps training center at Daytona Beach, Florida, as chief of the medical service. "Down there I had quite an experience with homesick girls determined to get out of the WACs and go home," he remembers. "Some of them had signed up after having quarrels with their sweethearts and now repented their rashness. Others had envisioned themselves in smart uniforms, driving cars for the colonels and generals, but instead had found themselves endlessly drilling on the hot sands. Often I'd find some of the girls weeping. They were nervous and emotionally upset, and sometimes I would have to send one home."

From Daytona Beach he was transferred to Camp Blanding, also in Florida, another tremendous army post. His duties were not lightened in this new assignment either. "I had an

[43]

out-patient clinic there. And some days," he recalls, "we'd treat two hundred to three hundred patients in that clinic. Anyone who wished could come to us for treatment, from a general's wife down, and we had to see the military men, too. Usually we could spend only a minute or two with each patient, and in that time we had to decide what to do with him, whether to send him to the hospital for an operation for appendicitis or treat him for hookworm or send him to the dentist or give him a box of pills or otherwise dispose of his case. The examining doctor, and that was I, hour after hour, day in and day out, had to make snap judgments, because always, it seemed, there were a hundred sitting out there in the waiting room, biding their turn to get in to see the doctor.

"There was a rule there at that time that the military personnel came first for treatment. A private came ahead of a general's wife. That was the rule. But it didn't always work out that way. I remember I had a nurse who had been in the WACs until they forced all nurses out of the WACs because they were needed in the Army as nurses. This girl was considerably disturbed because they transferred her to the Army, and she had decided that in carrying out her nursing assignments she would stick to the letter of the law. In that way, I believe she reasoned, she'd get even with the generals and the colonels who had been responsible for having her transferred. She would make the generals' and the colonels' wives wait their turn to see the doctor.

"Well, she knew the rule and that she was upholding it, though she also knew that in certain cases, particularly those of generals' wives, the rule was meant to be winked at. If the general's wife showed up at the clinic, the doctor was expected to see her at once. And this the WAC-turned-army nurse understood.

[44]

"One day I was seeing one patient after another when my telephone rang. I answered. It was the commanding general of the post on the other end. 'Major Cannon, what's the trouble that General So-and-So's wife can't get in to see you over there?' he inquired with some warmth.

" 'I'm sorry, General,' I replied. 'I didn't know she was waiting to see me.'

" 'Well,' he said, 'you take a look out there and see what's going on.'

"I went out into the waiting room, and there sat the general's wife near the foot of the line. The nurse had told her that she would have to wait until all the soldiers had been seen by the doctor.

"I took her into the office immediately. She had a little mole on her back that she wanted removed. I injected novocain and took it right off. And by the time the commanding general arrived at the clinic—I had suspected that he would come by to check—she was out and gone. The commanding officer was much happier, and so was I. The nurse, of course, had been right, technically. The general's wife hadn't been in pain and there had been no emergency, while a number of the enlisted men out there in the waiting room were actually suffering. But rules in the Army, as I said, aren't necessarily followed, particularly when generals' wives are concerned. That little nurse was about to get me in hot water."

At Blanding, Major Cannon was called up for examination for possible overseas duty assignment. At one point in the examination the examining physician asked the major to touch his toes without bending his knees. The major tried, but he couldn't reach below his knees. "Cannon, you shouldn't be in the Army, let alone be thinking of going overseas!" the doctor exclaimed. "I'm going to send you up to Atlanta General for a thorough examination. Man, you've got a bad back. It'll probably require surgery to fix it."

At Atlanta, Colonel Cannon (he had been promoted to lieutenant colonel as he was leaving Blanding) discovered he had a ruptured disc. The doctors wanted him to have two operations, six months apart, so that he would have been in a cast twelve months. "I couldn't face it," he said later. "I convinced them that it would be best to retire from the Army. I simply couldn't endure twelve months more in a cast; I remembered the intolerable claustrophobia from which I had suffered during my previous experience."

He was retired in the fall of 1946, after six years in the Army, with a disability classification. He might have remained in the service and become a full colonel in another two years or so, but he was never completely happy with army routine or restrictions.

Upon retiring he returned to Pickens, South Carolina, to re-establish himself in private practice. For several months he practiced from an office in his residence while he was building a small clinic, and in July 1947, when that structure was ready, he moved in. But he had hardly begun work in the clinic when again he began to have serious trouble with his back. He closed the office and went to Johns Hopkins Hospital. "I had an operation there for the ruptured disc, but it was a different procedure from the one they were planning to follow at Atlanta General," he explains. "Instead of being hospitalized twelve months I was required to stay there only twelve days and then to be on crutches for the next three months. I got back to work about November 1, and by early the next year began making plans for a hospital." Already he had added to his clinic a section out from the central part to provide space for a laboratory. When the hospital structure was built nearby, the laboratory became a connecting link between the clinic and the new building. With the completion of the construction work, Pickens had a hospital of which any community of comparable size might justly be proud.

Gaine Cannon's father had died in 1938, while his son was practicing in the Fayetteville community. "He was eighty-three, and had been active in his practice almost to the day of his death, which followed a cerebral hemorrhage. He delivered a baby a week before he died," his son recalls. "But I wasn't able to go home. I had several patients critically ill; two of them died, in fact, the day he did. Since I couldn't get anybody to look after my patients at that time, I felt I shouldn't leave. I knew that he would have felt the same way about it.

"My father, I'm happy to say, quickly forgave me for studying medicine in defiance of him. He let me know, in fact, that he was delighted that I had had the courage to defy him."

Until shortly before his death the elder Dr. Cannon had been going up into the mountains regularly on calls. Many Transylvania and Jackson County folk thought that he was the only doctor in the world, certainly the best; they had utter confidence in him and were devoted to him. Sometimes when he could not come to them, they would climb into a pickup truck or some other conveyance and ride all the way down to Pickens to have him treat them. Frequently in his later years he would go up to Rosman and reopen his little office, and from there he would have someone drive him (he never learned to drive an automobile) all over the mountain communities in which as a young physician he had ministered to his beloved mountain folk.

"He was a good doctor, and a greatly loved one," his son describes him. "The finest praise I ever get up here in the region where Father practiced is to have some old fellow whose aches and pains I have managed to ease say to me in utter sincerity, 'W'y, Doc, I 'low you're pretty nigh as good a doctor as yor pa was; not quite, o' course, but pretty nigh as good.' "

Gaine Cannon had named the Pickens hospital, a seventy-two-bed institution grown from the fourteen-bed clinic, the Cannon Memorial, not for himself but for his father. And after a few years of struggling to free the project of debt, including a loan of a hundred thousand dollars from the federal government, the hospital was debt-free and operating without loss. But Gaine Cannon again was nearing exhaustion.

"One day I saw one hundred and fourteen patients. That was unusually high, but it was not unusual to see from seventy to ninety a day and to make from ten to twenty house calls, most of them out in the country," he says of the Pickens era. "I had several examining rooms and would walk from room to room. I was always half dead from lack of sleep. To be allowed just to sleep, I thought, would be paradise. Sometimes I went to sleep, too, at the wrong time. I wrecked two automobiles by going to sleep and running off the shoulder. I shudder to think about it. I don't take chances now. When I get so sleepy I know I'm likely to nod, I pull off the road and take a nap. And often I get someone to drive for me and I pile up in the back seat and sleep as we are on the way to a patient's home and returning from the call."

At Pickens one of his physician friends warned Gaine Cannon, "You've got to stop practicing awhile and rest. And you can't rest if you stay here in Pickens. Go away someplace where your patients can't find you and can't telephone you, and just sit down and rock and rest. And don't come back for at least three months!"

Adding to his ordeal was the failure of Dr. Cannon's marriage. After having lived together for more than a decade and having had four children—David Gaine, Susan Melissa,

Priscilla Ann, and John Mark—Dr. Cannon and his wife began to see their interests diverging irreconcilably and they separated. When at length he discovered that their marriage had deteriorated beyond the level from which their living together might be resumed and happily continued, he sued for divorce. The lawsuit was tried, he was granted the divorce, and was given custody of the children. Shortly afterward his former wife remarried. Dr. Cannon, however, has remained single and his ascendant interest has been providing medical care for his people of the Balsam Grove community. Since in the breaking up of the home and the subsequent divorce Dr. Cannon was not in position to maintain a normal household for his children, who were quite young at the time, he permitted them to live with their mother. In the years succeeding they have occasionally visited him at Balsam Grove during periods when they were not in school, and one of the daughters with her infant son has spent a year with him at Balsam Grove during a part of the time that her husband was away in the armed services.

Dr. Cannon infrequently refers to his decade of married life, and when he does, succinctly and without bitterness he offers as one of the explanations of the failure of his marriage: "Everything was irregular. Too much hospital, she complained. That led to irregular hours, irregular meals, very little social life, which to her was of very considerable importance. She liked parties and dancing; I didn't. I wouldn't have liked that sort of life even if I'd had time for it. But I had no time. I was always seeing patients at the hospital or going on calls. We didn't have much normal family life."

With the ending of what family life he had had, his dedication to his professional duties, which he believes is the best way for him to make a vital contribution to the advancement of the Schweitzer philosophy of reverence for life, has become all but complete. Now his life has little resemblance to the routine of the usual physician. But there is no irregularity in his devotion to his philosophy. His reverence for life neither burgeons nor slackens; his allegiance, which is complete, is almost as regular as the wheeling of the planets.

Fortunately, especially now that his professional and personal burdens were heavy upon him, Gaine Cannon had a retreat to which he could go for relaxation and recuperation. Shortly after he settled at Pickens he had begun to go up into the Balsam Grove community. A friend, an Italian who operated a large lumber business at Rosman, also owned a considerable tract of land at Balsam Grove, including waterfalls on the river near the place where Shoal Creek flowed into it. Sometimes this man would ask the doctor to ride with him to the Balsam Grove area, and during one of these visits he told Gaine Cannon that a friend in Florida owned a large tract adjacent to his. This land included the property in the cove where the Albert Schweitzer Memorial Hospital later would be built, and on it were the farmhouse that would become the clinic and a few other small structures. Dr. Cannon expressed interest in buying some of that land, and his Italian friend interceded with the Florida owner to sell the doctor a small acreage. The man agreed, and some time later sold Dr. Cannon the entire property, which was almost five hundred acres.

So, Dr. Cannon recalls, when his doctor informed him that he would have to get away from Pickens and relax for at least three months, he immediately thought of the farmhouse. "I told myself that would be the perfect place for resting," he remembers. "It was about as isolated as a place could be. I'd just sit around and rock and listen to the creek rippling along past my front porch. I hadn't had any real vacation in years, and I was fagged out. I told myself I'd just take it easy, do nothing but sleep and eat and rock, and I wouldn't even rock fast.

"So I came up here and moved into the old house, which at that time was the only thing here in the flat except a ramshackle garage that later would become our obstetrics clinic. And I sat down to rock.

"Well, it worked out beautifully for a few days. Then the word began to spread around that there was a doctor living over there in the old house beside Shoal Creek, old Doc Cannon's boy, and the folk started coming. I saw them on the porch, I saw them in the living room, and it wasn't long until I was working harder and putting in more hours at it than I had been before I came up to Balsam Grove to rest. The mountain folk from miles around swarmed into our little cove. The upshot of it was that I had to go back to Pickens for the rest I had left Pickens to get. But I started coming back two days a week, Wednesdays and Sundays, and I practiced the other five days in Pickens; so during the week I had no day off. Nor have I had since, except now and then when I just up and ride off somewhere for a little while, including the period I spent with Dr. Schweitzer at Lambaréné—and I was working there, too.

"One Sunday morning in Balsam Grove I was awakened by a patient banging on the door. It was about four o'clock, I discovered when I got up. I was expecting to go back to bed when I saw him, so I just pulled on my trousers over my pajamas and slipped on my bedroom shoes. When I got back to my quarters, utterly weary, I had seen ninety-two patients and I still had on my pajamas and bedroom shoes. I had started before daylight, and now it was long past nightfall. I had my first food at nine o'clock that night. I had given, if I remember correctly, forty-two injections of one drug or another and I had written between seventy-five and eighty prescriptions, and examined and checked the blood pressures of all ninety-two patients."

Dr. Cannon's returning two days a week to Balsam Grove troubled him, however, because it left his patients in Pickens unattended on those days. And soon the Balsam Grove folk were pleading with him to spend more days in the mountains, and now and then on the days he was in Pickens he would receive a call from the Balsam Grove community urging him to come see some critically ill patient in an isolated cove deep in the hills. He was in a dilemma:

"I didn't know what to do. The pace was becoming more frenzied week by week. I had been overworked in Pickens before I had gone up to Balsam Grove, and now I had extended my territory into a tremendous area in the Transylvania and Jackson counties region up in the North Carolina Blue Ridge.

"Then by good fortune I met Dr. Clarence Edens. He was a godsend.

"Dr. Edens was living at Easley, South Carolina, a small town about eight miles southeast of Pickens. He had just resigned from a year's service in public health work and had not resumed private practice. Also a veteran of World War II, he, too, had tired of the regimented life of an army doctor, and had gone into the public health service because it seemed to offer a less restricted routine. Now back in his home town, he had decided to settle there permanently. He was a native of Pickens County, born in the late afternoon shadow of Table Rock, on the South Carolina-North Carolina state line, and my father had been the Edens family's doctor when Clarence Edens was a child. He told me of an incident that happened when he was a very small boy, one that involved my father. Father had been passing the Edens home and had stopped a moment to chat with Mr. Edens, who was out in the front yard. The elder Edens had invited Father in to dinner and Father, as was his custom, had gone into the house without taking his hat off. When he started into the dining room with his hat still on, four-year-old Clarence was shocked. 'Say, mister,' he asked, 'don't you think you ought to take your hat off?' Whereupon my father, grinning, agreed. 'Yes, son,' he said, 'I think that would be a good idea.' And he removed the hat. He hadn't realized, of course, that he was wearing it.

"Dr. Edens, the thought came to me, was the very man I needed to help me at Balsam Grove. I would see if I could persuade him to go up there on the days I was in Pickens and stay in Pickens when I was at Balsam Grove. I made the proposal, and he was agreeable. So we worked out arrangements, and Dr. Edens came up to Balsam Grove and stayed almost continuously for about three months. Then we began alternating our days at Balsam Grove and Pickens. Later Dr. Edens opened an office in Easley, but he continued to help me at Balsam Grove, and he still does a large part of his time. He's a good doctor; he knows his medicine. But perhaps of equal importance in assuring him success in the Balsam Grove community, the people like him. They know that he is warmly interested in them, and he understands them and their problems. He also believes in the Schweitzer philosophy of reverence for life, and that means much to me. Recently in an effort to serve the hospital even more efficiently in the future, Dr. Edens has been taking special work in anesthetization. He's a great asset to our hospital and to the community."

CHAPTER

6

THE rush of Balsam Grove folk to the farmhouse at the turning of Shoal Creek did not abate in the weeks that followed Gaine Cannon's arrival there. In fact, as it became known about the community and over in Jackson County that a doctor was spending two days a week there, more patients drove into the little cove. The ninety-two he treated on one Sunday were the largest group seen on any one day, but regularly sixty to seventy on Sundays and forty to fifty on Wednesdays came to his improvised clinic.

About the time Dr. Cannon began going up to Balsam Grove twice a week (this was in 1953) a community development program was beginning to make headway in western North Carolina. This program provided competition among the communities in a campaign of general improvement. One day a committee from Balsam Grove came to Dr. Cannon's and asked him if he would have his mailbox painted, put his name on it, and do a few other small chores to make the place more attractive as his part in the effort to improve the neighborhood. Dr. Cannon agreed and pledged his help in any way he might contribute to the program, and during the conversation one of the committee members suggested that he establish a small clinic in Balsam Grove.

"That's when the idea of a hospital there was born," he says. He recalls those beginning days:

"From the suggestion that we establish a clinic, I conceived the idea of developing such a clinic into a little community hospital. We talked it back and forth, and everybody seemed pleased with the notion that we might be able to build one, so we had a meeting at the schoolhouse to discuss the proposal and see if the folk really wanted a hospital and if they thought we would be able to establish it.

"They were enthusiastic in their support of the proposal, and their enthusiasm inspired me to envision big things for the community, all of them centered around a hospital that would serve an increasingly expanding circle of mountain country. That was late in the fall of 1953. Perhaps it's a good thing that I didn't foresee then that we would be ten years building the hospital and that for those ten years we would have only the farmhouse-clinic, the old garage converted into a two-story obstetrics building, the old barn across the creek, which we use mainly for storage, and four small residential buildings I have added, including my apartment at the base of the hill, seventy-five steps across the cove from the clinic. Maybe if I'd known then that our dream would be a whole decade in becoming a reality, I would have been less enthusiastic.

"But that night at the schoolhouse I proposed that we set a goal for our project, and that we aspire to high accomplishment. And to show the people that we were planning to do big things, I suggested we give our little hospital a big name. They agreed, and asked me to propose one. I suggested that we call it the Albert Schweitzer Memorial Hospital.

"Few of those folk at the meeting had ever heard of Albert Schweitzer. But they approved of the name; certainly it sounded big enough. I told them that I would write to Dr. Schweitzer and ask his permission to use his name.

"Our little improvement association had $5.35 in the treasury. The money was appropriated to the fund for building a hospital. At my suggestion it was also agreed that each patient coming to our clinic should bring two good, solid, rounded river stones on each visit to the doctor. The folk began bringing stones, two and three, sometimes a pickup load of them, along with a sick wife or sick baby or even a sick husband, and before long we had a pile of building stones as large as a freight car. We took pictures of patients handing me stones and pictures of the great pile, and these we sent to Dr. Schweitzer, at Lambaréné. Soon we had a reply giving us permission to name our hospital for him and expressing his delight that we were undertaking such a project.

Accompanying the letter from Dr. Schweitzer was a translation of it by Mrs. Anna Hausknecht, one of the important people at Lambaréné. A note from Mrs. Hausknecht observes:

"Dr. Schweitzer thinks his handwriting tired. He suffers frequently from the writer's cramp."

Then she translates the Schweitzer letter:

Dear Doctor Cannon, I cannot but contemplate the picture on which you are occupied with a heap of stones, because, since my return to Lambaréné in the end of 1954, I did the same. I have built a village for 250 leper patients, and this means a constant trouble to have stones enough. Here, I have to dig the stones out of the soil between palm trees and I have to stay with the workers, so that our natives do not sit down to tell stories, but go on digging. So you are a man with whom I deal the trouble for stones. I thank you cordially for your very lovely letter. How

[56]

courageous you are to build two hospitals during your life. I know well what that means. I built twice my hospital, first before 1914, the second time after the first world war, between 1925 and 1927. And at present as an old man, the village for the leper patients. I always built together with primitive natives, who had no notion of it at all and possessed a minimum of zeal for working. So I can evaluate what your two hospitals may cost as work and nerves. To express the community between you and me, you give your second hospital my name. I appreciate the honor and sympathy you bestow upon me. I thank you from heart. If from time to time you give me some news about the construction, it would be a joy for me. How fine it would be, if one day we could meet one another somewhere. Will this be realizable?

With fond thoughts,
Yours devoted,
Albert Schweitzer

"That letter is among my most prized possessions. I immediately had it framed and hung it on the wall in the clinic's reception room. When the hospital building, then but a dream and a growing mound of stones, was finished and occupied, I would give it and a large picture of Dr. Schweitzer the most prominent position in the lobby.

"So, with Dr. Schweitzer's approval of our request to name the hospital for him and with an accumulating supply of building stones, but little money, we Balsam Grove folk set to work. I deeded the necessary site to the hospital, and we began digging the foundation trenches. I had drawn the building plans myself after consultation with an architect and building contractors. I designed the structure to have a large central section, with wings running off from each side at a slight angle. We graded back the slope, which at some points came steeply down from the high hill behind the building site. Boys and girls from the Scout troops of the community helped with the digging; they pushed wheelbarrows of dirt and wielded picks and shovels. We had strung electric lights about the place and often worked at night.

"In addition to giving the site I had agreed to provide all the cinder blocks needed for the inner side of the stone walls and also to employ all the skilled labor required in the construction."

Through the intervening decade from 1953, the work has proceeded, with frequent long interruptions. But Dr. Cannon has been doing more than providing the skilled labor, including the stone setters, and the cinder blocks, cement, and mortar. As the outside of the hospital recently neared completion, he estimated that he has contributed some thirty thousand dollars in cash, in excess of the cost of the materials and the skilled labor employed. The outlay in money, he further estimated, has been double that amount, perhaps as much as seventy-five thousand dollars, including his contributions, in addition to probably forty thousand man-hours contributed by the Balsam Grove folk. Over the ten years the building has been under construction, therefore, between six thousand and seventy-five hundred dollars have been contributed yearly, on an average, out of fees earned by the doctor and contributions in the main from the people in the community. And since the doctor's fees are paid principally by Balsam Grove folk, almost all the money has come from that immediate section of the mountains, though occasionally certain organizations and the doctor's friends in various parts of the nation have helped.

"We have been working at the project as fast as we have been able," Dr. Cannon says, "and our community has looked forward to the day when we would have the building finished, equipped, and in operation. Our Balsam Grove folk have been watching proudly as their building has advanced a little every few weeks and they point happily to the sign down on the highway directing the motorist to the Albert Schweitzer Memorial Hospital. They heartily approve our selection of a name.

"But few outsiders, seeing the sign as they pass along the road or as they venture the half mile up the lane to the hospital itself, understand.

"The Albert Schweitzer Memorial Hospital in North Carolina? In the North Carolina mountains? Why? Why should a little mountain hospital in North Carolina be named for Albert Schweitzer?"

Such questions invariably are asked by visitors to Balsam Grove.

But no one who knows Gaine Cannon (and certainly no resident of that region is better known) asks such questions. His friends understand.

"And when I tell anybody who does ask me why I named my hospital for Dr. Schweitzer that I did it simply because of my great admiration for this man, then he at once wants to know why and how I became such an admirer of Dr. Schweitzer."

The story that Gaine Cannon tells in answer to such questions goes back three decades, and says he, it came about this way:

"When I finished my premedical training with graduation from Berea College, in Kentucky, in 1925, I was unsettled —in fact, greatly disturbed—about my religious beliefs or lack of them. I simply could not accept the orthodoxy of various denominations, because there were in the creeds of these churches so many statements of belief that I could not agree with. I could not give up the idea of God, of a Supreme Power, yet I could not believe in the God that many of my friends professed to believe in. I just could not square my beliefs with the literal account in the Bible of Adam and Eve, for example, and Jonah and the whale and the Old Testament stories of God's killing pagan peoples or instructing His Jewish children to destroy them. The idea that a merciful and loving Father could do such horrible things was repugnant to me, and I felt that such a God—and I still do— was not the God of the noble and loving young man of Galilee.

"So whether my views about the orthodox churches were correct or not, I was troubled and I couldn't get in the creeds of those churches the answers to my problems, even though I did not then and do not now doubt the existence of a good and all-powerful Creator and Ruler of life. I don't see how anyone, in fact, who claims to be a scientist or has even a rudimentary knowledge of science can be an atheist. I don't see how anyone could possibly believe that this amazingly wonderful and intricate universe could have evolved out of chance and accident."

During the period that he was finishing college and going through medical school, Gaine Cannon continued to be troubled. He was searching vainly for something that would sustain him, that he could reconcile with his own developing philosophy or that would be a philosophy upon which he could rest untroubled and at peace. He tells how he came upon what he was seeking:

"One day while I was interning, still adrift so far as my religious experience was concerned and quite unhappy about it, I happened to pick up a little magazine, and in it I discovered an article titled 'The Jungle Doctor.' I began reading it casually, but I quickly became interested. That was in 1931. And from then on I read everything I could find that Albert Schweitzer had written and that had been written about him. He grew on me, especially his reverence for life, which I took to be his philosophy of life. And this not only became my own philosophy but it became also my way of life. And as I began to be deeply concerned about other people and other living things and came to think in terms of their wills to live and about my search to find a way out of doubt and despair into confidence and hope and peace, I began to feel this doubt and darkness lifting and light and peace calming my troubled thoughts. This then, I told myself, is what I want, what I need, what I have been searching for. Albert Schweitzer in his way of life, in his reverence for all life, has shown me the way, and I feel now that I will need little else if I live up to this sincerely and truthfully practice it, call it philosophy or religion or way of life or what you may. Some persons have defined it as the essence of Christianity, as the way of life of Jesus of Galilee, and it seems to me that it is. But however that may be, it sustains me. And that is how I became such an admirer of Albert Schweitzer."

That, too, was the basis of the renewal and strengthening of Gaine Cannon's interest in his people of the mountains, as he describes them with unfeigned affection, "these wonderfully unspoiled Americans." Albert Schweitzer, he invariably hastens to point out, gave up several careers of potentially unlimited promise before he became a doctor of medicine and went far away from relatives, friends, and everything he had keenly enjoyed and appreciated to live in the equatorial jungles of Africa and to minister to what the world considered black savages but who to him were his brothers, the children of God.

"If Albert Schweitzer could go into the steaming jungles of Africa to minister to the bodies and souls of ignorant and savage black men, then certainly I could go into my native mountains and minister to the bodies, and perhaps in some measure to the souls, of fellow Americans who needed my help. So to Albert Schweitzer I give much of the credit, if credit it be, for our establishing a little hospital in the hills, and to the hospital happily and out of deep devotion I gave his name."

Gaine Cannon's devotion to Dr. Schweitzer, his reverence for the man, approaches worship. As he treats patients in the clinic or goes into mountain homes on the steep hillsides or in the secluded coves he talks to anyone who will listen of the work at Lambaréné and of the Schweitzer philosophy. Standing in his little kitchen, sipping soup and munching crackers during a ten-minute respite from his waiting room filled with patients, or in the late evening, perhaps long past midnight, his large frame sprawled in a chair facing the television set and a program being largely ignored, Dr. Cannon is happiest when he is expounding upon Schweitzer and his reverence for life. Perhaps few Americans are as familiar with the course of the famous European's career as the North Carolina doctor; none is a more devoted disciple.

"When he was a very young man Albert Schweitzer promised himself he would give his life until he was thirty to philosophy, theology, music, and writing," Dr. Cannon will reveal, "and after that he would devote it to something of more direct service to mankind, something he could do with his hands as well as his brains and heart. So when he was about thirty-eight, he earned his Doctor of Medicine degree. Earlier he had been the recipient of a Doctor of Philosophy degree, and some years afterward he had the degree of Doctor of

Theology conferred upon him. He is a doctor in two other fields also, Doctor of Laws and Doctor of Music, and also Doctor of Divinity.

"He studied medicine in the expectation of going to Africa to practice. As a child he had seen a statue of a Negro slave lying frightened and cowering at the feet of his white master, and this statue had made a powerful impression upon him. I like to ponder the contribution that sculptor made in ultimately giving Albert Schweitzer to medicine and to Africa. At any rate, seeing that statue gave the little Alsatian boy the idea, 'Here will be my work,' the idea to go back to the black man's country and do what he could to repay him for the injustice that had been done him through the long years. And the idea remained with him, and grew. So when he had completed his medical studies and earned his Doctor of Medicine degree, he made plans to go to Africa."

Dr. Schweitzer went out to Lambaréné, in the Gabon region of French Equatorial Africa, in 1913. He had been there twenty years before Gaine Cannon first read about him. It would be almost thirty years after he read "The Jungle Doctor" before he would see Schweitzer. But in the years between he would read and collect everything Dr. Schweitzer published and every book written about him, as far as he was able to discover, and countless articles. And the more Gaine Cannon has studied the works of the famous doctor of the African jungles, the more he has sought to comprehend what Schweitzer means by his *Ehrfurcht vor dem Leben*," the more he has tried to translate Schweitzer's philosophy into a way of life for himself; in ministering to his beloved folk of the mountains, Gaine Cannon feels that he is doing work in some ways comparable to the work being done at Lambaréné, even though it is less dramatic and is being done for persons far less isolated and underprivileged than those Africans with whom Dr. Schweitzer is expending his life of devoted service.

Dr. Cannon's dedication to his work in the mountain region, like Dr. Schweitzer's to the natives of the Gabon area, does not permit him the orderly life of the average city or suburban doctor.

"My office hours are day and night throughout the week," he says. "And that's the only way it can be for a mountain doctor doing general practice. People come to see the doctor when they can, or they wait until they find someone who can take the message that they want the doctor to visit them. They can't walk fifty miles or so and many of them have no other way of traveling except on foot. So they have to wait until the return of the pickup that's hauling pulpwood or firewood to market, or they must wait until a neighbor who is working in town gets home, and generally that is after dark, and maybe long after dark if it's in the wintertime. Then they eat supper and start out to see the doctor. It may take them hours to get here over mountain trails. If I worked only regular hours, many of my patients would never be able to see me.

"I think that's one of the troubles now with doctors over the country, in the cities particularly, and to a large extent even in the villages. They try to do their doctoring as if they were running a bank or a store. Office hours, nine to five, say. And that's no way to do it, the way I understand the ethics of the profession. People don't get sick by the clock; they don't have babies by the clock. They get sick any hour of the twenty-four, and the way I look at it, a good doctor goes any time and anywhere he is needed. And in my opinion, that applies to doctors in cities.

"Maybe a man has worked hard all day, cutting and hauling pulpwood or at our cigarette paper plant over at Brevard or at one of the scores of hard tasks in our nearby communities, and he comes home tired and all but worn out to find a sick wife or sick baby. So he bundles up the sick wife or baby and he brings the ill one over to Balsam Grove. He may not get here until ten or eleven o'clock, or maybe after midnight. Now, wouldn't I be a poor doctor and a sorry neighbor if I refused to treat the sick one, if I sent somebody out to his truck or car to tell him that I was sorry but my office hours had ended for the day? What sort of a doctor or good neighbor would I be if someone drove into our grounds at midnight and told me that his father or son or wife or mother or baby was suffering terribly and I refused to return with him to see what I could do for the sufferer, even though the call might keep me out the remainder of the night? I'll tell you this: if I refused to see such folk and do my utmost to help them, regardless of the inconvenience or discomfort to me, I would be unworthy of bearing the title of doctor; I would say that I was disgracing my honored profession. I realize that many doctors nowadays don't look at it that way, but I surely do. I look at it just the same way my old mountain-doctor father did."

Frequently a patient who has aroused Dr. Cannon out of a sound sleep or to whose home the doctor has struggled through mud or sleet or snow after being summoned there by a neighbor after midnight will say to him, "Doc, if you can, won't you give me a shot? I ain't got no money to have no 'script' filled." Most of his patients refer to prescriptions as "scripts."

"Medicine will serve you better than a shot," the doctor will reply. "And you won't have to have a prescription filled; I've got the medicine right here."

"But, Doc, I ain't got no money to pay for no medicine, neither."

"Who's asked you to pay for it?" Dr. Cannon will reply. "Whether you have the money or not, it makes no difference. We've never turned anybody away because he didn't have the money to pay for a call or for medicine, have we?"

"If you have, Doc, well now, I ain't never aheared tell 'bout it."

"We never turn anybody away," the doctor will assure him. "We'll give you the medicine." And Dr. Cannon frequently will make a follow-up call without payment for either the call or the medicine.

"That works a hardship on us," says the doctor, "because it's difficult to get money to replace medicines we give away. Right now, for instance, among the pressing needs is a fund from which to buy these medicines that we will provide without cost to patients who can't pay for them. Somehow we have managed to find the money." Much of this money comes from Dr. Cannon's own pocket, and he knows it will probably never be repaid. "I don't make very much money," he will explain, "and most of that goes to the fund for building the hospital. I see a large number of patients, but I can't demand large fees, even if I were of a mind to, and I'm not. But we pick up a little money in side lines, like selling candy and various knickknacks to patients and visitors, mountain souvenirs, and such trinkets, and occasionally friends from over the country send us a little check for our work. So we have been able to keep going, and slowly the hospital building has been coming along.

"But though we don't make much money, certainly as compared with the big-city specialist, we get paid for it in reality. The fact that I give medicine to a poor fellow or some old woman or an ailing child that helps the patient, maybe cures him of his ailment, is for me payment enough. I don't expect to get any further payment, and often I don't. But sometimes I do. It makes little difference to me, though, because I get paid right then. Dr. Schweitzer says that one should never do anything expecting something in return. Don't expect to be repaid, he insists, don't expect something in return for what you have done. If it's not needed, don't do it; if it is needed, do it and forget about repayment. It'll usually come back to you in one way or another, I have found through the years. But don't look for it. Do it because there's a need for it. I'm anything but a theologian, but there are some verses in Matthew in which Jesus is quoted as saying substantially this: 'If a man sues you in court and takes away your coat, let him have your cloak also. And whoever compels you to go a mile with him, go with him two miles.'

"Now, to my way of thinking, that is the gist of Dr. Schweitzer's philosophy, and it's mine. That is going the second mile. And when you go the second mile, I've discovered in doing it, there's even greater joy in going the third mile."

CHAPTER

7

ONE of Dr. Gaine Cannon's first discoveries after coming from Pickens to the Balsam Grove community was that many of his patients of about his age or a few years older had been given the first name Cannon. Yet his father had had no relatives of the Cannon name in that section. Gaine Cannon surmised correctly that the parents of these first-name Cannons had named them for the beloved mountain doctor who had brought them into the world.

But one day when he met a bearded patriarch who lived a little way down the road from him and discovered that his name was Cannon McCall, the doctor's curiosity was aroused. How did it happen that this old man had been given the name Cannon?

"Look here, Cannon," the doctor said to him some weeks later, after he felt that the old man's natural suspicion of strangers had been overcome, "I've been wondering where you got that name Cannon. I know you must have known my father, but I figure you're a little too old for him to have delivered you."

"Yes, Doc—that's right," the patriarch agreed. He talked

with a rasping, weak voice, and his words came out jerkily, three or four at a time, then a pause, and three or four more. "My name it—was Albert—till I was—nine year old—but then my folks, they—liked yor pappy so well—that they decided to—call me Cannon—fer him. So I been Cannon—McCall ever since."

Cannon McCall quickly became one of Dr. Cannon's favorite mountain folk. He liked to talk with him and Aunt Corrie, his wife, and he also got to know Vernon.

Cannon has five or six boys, long, lanky fellows, like those mountaineers sometimes seen in *Esquire* cartoons, showing them stretched out under the trees, long-whiskered and barefoot, with their coon dogs and their gallon jugs of white lightning beside them. Vernon is the third or fourth son of Cannon and Aunt Corrie. "He's one of the three or four who live with the old folk," Gaine Cannon says, "and he's skinny and emaciated. He also drinks heavily." And although the consequences of Vernon's alcoholism are tragic they have also caused some bizarre moments for Cannon's staff.

There are many tales to tell about Vernon, but the most extraordinary story involving him must be the one that Peggy Cowart tells. Peggy lives in Florida, where her husband owns a large cattle ranch and has other business enterprises. But her mother's people were from this Transylvania region, and when she and her husband decided to build a summer home in the mountains they selected Balsam Grove as the location for it. Their home, in fact, is near the old house in which the McCalls were then living; Peggy knows Cannon McCall and his wife and their lanky sons, particularly Vernon. She is an experienced and capable nurse. Frequently she helps at the hospital, especially when the doctor's regular nurse, Helen McCall, is not on duty.

[69]

One night a few summers ago Peggy was at home alone; her husband had not come up from Florida. It was about three o'clock in the morning when she was awakened by a noise at the back door. There was an electric light on a post in the yard, and by this light, when she slipped to her window, she could see a man at the door.

"Don't move! I've got a gun on you!" she called out. "Walk over into the light where I can see you!"

"Don't shoot, Paggy!" the back-door visitor shouted. "It's just old John!" The mountain folk call her "Paggy." And when Vernon is drunk he calls himself "Dr. Cannon" and usually anybody else "John."

"Vernon, what in thunder are you doing at my house this time of night?" Peggy demanded.

But instead of answering, Vernon ran. Peggy heard him flatfooting it across the lawn toward the little river, which is the north fork of the French Broad; the stream runs some forty or fifty yards in front of her house. There is a small cat-walk across the stream, about three feet above the water, and in a moment she heard Vernon's feet hit that catwalk. In the next instant there was a terrific splash. Vernon had fallen into the water.

Peggy herself takes up the story:

"I jumped from the bed—I'd just sat down on it when Vernon started running—stuck my feet into my bedroom slippers, and went racing for the river. Vernon was splashing about, yelling and screaming. I just knew he was drunk and would drown if I didn't get to him quickly. The water was deep enough there to be over his head, and I was sure Vernon couldn't swim even when sober.

"I was wearing a pair of summer shorty pajamas, and I hadn't paused to throw on a robe. I just struck out, without another thought than that Vernon would be drowned if I didn't get to him in a hurry. And when I got down there, Vernon was praying in a high, nasal pleading, literally to high heaven. 'O Lord, don't let it start arainin',' he was begging.

"Well, I got him out. He was a skinny fellow and not very heavy, and we splashed and jumped until we reached the bank. There was an old log there, and we sat down on it and I brushed the water out of my eyes and pushed my hair back. 'Vernon,' I said to him when I'd recovered my breath, 'would you please tell me what you were doing here at my house at this time of morning?'

" 'Paggy, I'm adyin',' he said in his most pitiful tone. 'Old John's adyin'. He's adyin' for sure, Paggy. And I come up here to git you to pray for me. That's what I come for, to git you to pray for me, and I wants you to do it.'

" 'Vernon, if you needed a shot or a pill or something like that,' I told him, 'I could help you. But praying for you is sort of out of my line. I don't think I'd be very good at that.'

" 'Now, don't talk that away, Paggy,' he pleaded. 'I told Mama that you're the best woman in Gloucester'—Gloucester is the name of the little section where we lived—'and I wanted you to pray for me.'

"Vernon kept pleading with me to pray for him. 'Please pray for me, Paggy. John's adyin'. Sure as hell's fire, Paggy, old John, he's adyin'.' I knew that despite the soaking in that very cold water Vernon was still pretty drunk because he was calling himself John.

" 'Well, O.K., Vernon,' I said to him when I saw that he was determined, 'I'll pray for you the best I can.' So we knelt down beside the log, for he wanted to kneel. 'O Lord, look down on this poor soul, and—' Then I started laughing. I didn't mean to be sacrilegious, but it just suddenly struck me how funny it must be to the Lord looking down on Vernon and me—Vernon drunk and half drowned and me soaking-wet in shorty pajamas and with my hair streaming, kneeling there beside a log by the riverbank in the middle of the night. But I quickly apologized. 'I'm sorry, Vernon. I oughtn't to have done that.'

" 'That's all right, Paggy,' he assured me. 'Just go ahead and shout. I just love it!' He thought that I had been shouting."

Vernon's mother, Aunt Corrie McCall, as all Balsam Grove calls her, is one of Dr. Cannon's most beloved elder citizens of the community and one of its most interesting ones. Gaine Cannon delights in telling a story about her also told him by Peggy Cowart:

"Once when I was driving past her house, Aunt Corrie flagged me down.

" 'Paggy,' she said when I stopped the car, 'I want you to take my blood.'

"I told her I would, but explained that she'd have to let me take her to the hospital, where we had needles, syringes, and test tubes.

" 'No, Paggy,' she declared, 'that ain't what I'm atalkin' 'bout. Ain't you got one of them there sashes what you wrops 'round yor arm?'

" 'Yes, I have,' I said, understanding then what she meant, 'and I have it here in the car.' She wasn't wanting a blood test; she was wanting me to take her blood pressure—'prassure,' they call it up here. So I went with her to her house and sat on the front porch while I took her blood pressure. As I was about to finish, she suddenly spoke out excitedly.

" 'Paggy, you know what I just heared?'

" 'No. What, Aunt Corrie?'

" 'I heared there was eight Jeeploads o' Confederate lawyers cut loose in Middle Fork.'

"I didn't know what she was talking about, of course, but I saw that she was perturbed. 'Well, are they doing much damage, Aunt Corrie?' I asked her.

" 'I reckon to God they are, honey,' the old lady declared with fervor, but with no thought of irreverence. 'They cut five stills this mornin'.'

"What she was trying to tell me, I discovered afterward, was that eight—not eight Jeeploads, but eight men riding in Jeeps—eight government revenue officers, eight federal lawmen rather than Confederate lawyers, had located and cut up five moonshine stills. But Aunt Corrie had more news to tell me about that raid. 'Yes, Paggy,' she said, 'they cut five stills this mornin' and they got two of yor cousins!' And the revenuers had indeed, I learned for certain later."

But although Dr. Cannon delights in telling stories and laughing heartily about the ludicrous doings of his neighbors in Balsam Grove and enjoys their sometimes strange usage of words and treatment of the language, he never laughs at them. "I only laugh with them. You don't laugh *at* mountain people. And why should I? They are my folk, and they are the finest people in the world, the very salt of the earth. I would never be completely happy away from them. Many people not of the mountains, including good personal friends of mine, who have spent time with them and come to know and appreciate their sterling worth, agree.

"Yet now and then we'll have a visitor to the hills who reveals a patronizing attitude, which is quickly sensed—and not appreciated—by our mountain folk. Such a person may be amused to hear certain expressions that he concludes are simply the talk of illiterates. But he himself is really the illiterate one in not knowing that these words are survivals, in a community until recently isolated from the world of changing language, of that English spoken and written in Eliza-

[73]

bethan England. Such a word, for example, is *ferninst*, meaning over against, close to, beside.

" 'Where' bouts will I find the cow chain?'

" 'Ahangin' on that air post over there ferninst the corn crib.' "

But all strange words, or words strangely used or pronounced, don't go back to good Queen Bess. One day while Dr. Cannon was away on a call, one of the women of Balsam Grove came to the clinic. It happened that the doctor had left Peggy Cowart to stand in for him. Upon his return she told him about the woman's visit.

"Paggy," this woman had said to the nurse, "have you got something for an upsot stomach?"

"Well, I might give you something to relieve you until Dr. Cannon gets back," Peggy told her. "Have you been vomiting?"

"No," she answered, "I ain't."

"Does your stomach hurt?"

"Yes, good heavens it does!"

"Any diarrhea?"

"No, I ain't got nothin' like that."

"Are you constipated?"

She shook her head. "No, Paggy, I'd say my bowels is right reverent."

"The good woman," Dr. Cannon hastened to explain, "didn't mean, of course, that the particular area of her anatomy inquired about was possessed of a pious or even respectful attitude, but rather that its functions were being performed in *regular* manner."

Although in his practice Dr. Cannon regularly encounters unusual words as well as the novel usage of familiar words and phrases, he is fearful that within two or three generations in the mountains almost all of this picturesque language will have been irretrievably lost.

"It has survived only because of the isolation of our region," he explains. "Two centuries ago settlers coming to America from England and Scotland pushed westward into the mountains, bringing with them the language of their day. And geography kept them there; there was little going and coming. Until recent years, the last three or four decades, in fact, there were few roads back into the hills, and generation after generation lived and died in inaccessible coves with hardly any contact with the outside world. So they maintained their way of life, including their language, virtually intact, while in the melting pot of the world beyond everything was changing, particularly language.

"But today it would be difficult, doubtless impossible, to find a truly isolated community in North Carolina. Great hard-surfaced highways sweep over causeways and across long steel-and-concrete bridges to the Outer Banks on the Atlantic coast and far westward swing along the crest of the Blue Ridge and the Great Smokies, and push down into the flatlands and the valleys to enmesh the one hundred county seats and innumerable cities, towns, villages, farms, and forests into one increasingly homogeneous commonwealth. The isolation of the old days is gone forever."

The doctor further points out that the largest transportation system in the world, the North Carolina public school buses traveling millions of passenger miles every week to transport children to schools in every large community in the state, has effectively ended isolation. The schools themselves have so stirred and mixed and rounded these pupils that, some citizens already are insisting, the product is soon likely to become a stereotype lacking the delightful individuality of its various forebears. Television antennas sticking above mountain cabins and seashore shacks, too, like those raised smugly atop fashionable country club estate homes and row on row of standard one-stories in suburban, closely huddled subdivisions, bring in Washington and London and Moscow and Paris along with the pabulum of Westerns and detective mysteries and moronic serials and a flood *ad nauseam* of laxatives, detergents, and deodorants.

But although they must surely do it, consolidated schools and diesel-powered tractor-trailers bringing in television sets and freezers and hi-fi record players, and rural electrification lines and penicillin and even a newly built satellite tracking station, have not been able completely to drive out of Balsam Grove some of the more prevalent and persistent superstitions.

"And I haven't attempted to dispel them," Dr. Cannon says. "In fact, sometimes I even employ a patient's firm belief in a certain superstition as an aid in treating his ailment. And I never speak disparagingly of anyone's beliefs."

A girl in Balsam Grove, for example, came to see Dr. Cannon one day with an annoying case of poison ivy. She was a high school pupil, though her language did not indicate it.

"I should've knowed better, Doctor," she declared. "I was just awalkin' along and my little sister was awalkin' along with me, and when I seen it I was afraid she'd get in it, and I p'inted to it to warn her to keep away from it, and you know ap'intin' at it is worse than even arubbin' in it."

"Well, I've got some stuff here that will stop the itching and dry it up," the doctor told her. "Put a little of it on the rash places every now and then and pretty soon it will be gone." Then to assure the girl that he was not scornful of her belief about the danger of pointing to a poison ivy vine, he added, "It might be a good idea hereafter to try to remember not to point at it or get near it when you happen to see a patch of poison ivy or poison oak."

Mountain folk have a strong sense of personal pride and dignity. "If she had got the notion that I was making fun of her idea about 'p'intin' at poison ivy," Dr. Cannon explains, "she would have been hurt and perhaps offended. Very likely she would have refused to use the ointment I gave her. So I always try to agree with my patients if I can when their superstitions aren't opposed to good medical practice, and thereby get their co-operation in following my instructions."

An even more interesting superstition persists in some of the homes in the Balsam Grove community and farther back into the hills surrounding it. It is the belief that to cure asthma in a child one must nail up a stick for the sufferer. This is the way it works, and say those who do not doubt its efficacy, the procedure must be followed meticulously if a cure is to be achieved.

When a youngster has asthma, a member of his family must cut a certain kind of stick—whether from a black gum or sweet gum, the doctor is not certain—and the child must stand with his back to the wall and hold the stick parallel with the floor and as high above his head as he can reach. The stick is then nailed to the wall at that point. When the little asthma sufferer has grown so that the top of his head touches the stick, the asthma will go away; he will be cured.

"Many of our mountain people believe firmly in the nailed-up-stick cure," Dr. Cannon says. "So when I go into a home where they have a stick nailed to the wall for a child suffering with asthma, I never under any circumstances speak lightly of this practice. Yet of course I want to help the little victim. So generally I refer to the stick on the wall. 'You know,' I'll say, 'there are some cures handed down by the old folk that

I don't put much stock in. But I do in this asthma stick. I'd advise anybody who has a child with asthma to have a stick nailed up, just so they're sure not to nail it too high. They oughtn't to let the child stretch or stand on tiptoe, but just reach up comfortable and flat-footed, and then nail it right there. I've seen this work many a time.'

"But if the child I have come to see is having difficulty, and he usually is or they wouldn't have sent for me, I'll say something like this: 'Now I'm sure that this stick method will work, but in the meantime I think it might be a good idea to help it along a little with some temporary treatment until he grows up to the stick.'"

The parents are then quite willing for Dr. Cannon to treat the child. And after several months of "temporary" treatment the child has considerably improved; by the time he grows up to the stick, he probably will have overcome the disorder.

"The thing about this stick cure for asthma is that most children naturally outgrow asthma, and by the time a child's head reaches the stick he is well. But I would never dare tell a parent who believed in this stick business, who was convinced that the stick itself had something to do with driving away the asthma, that there was no efficacy in that treatment."

This stick-nailed-to-the-wall cure for asthma is in the same general category of superstitions as the cure for warts in which many of the mountain folk, as well as persons in many other sections of the nation, have great faith. If you have a wart, this method of cure prescribes, you must scratch it with a pin or needle, or even the blade of a pocketknife, until it bleeds. Then you rub a grain of corn into the blood from the wart and feed the grain to a black chicken. You must be sure that the chicken is completely black. A Rhode Island Red, for instance, would never do; every feather must be black. And soon after the black chicken swallows the corn, the wart will most certainly go away.

"That treatment generally works, too," Dr. Cannon agrees. "But warts usually disappear after a time anyway, just as the child's asthma is likely to be cured by the time he reaches a certain age. But here again I wouldn't think of telling a patient that his feeding a black chicken the wart-bloodied grain of corn had had nothing to do with the wart's going away."

Many of Dr. Cannon's patients in the Blue Ridge Mountains (and persons down in the Piedmont and the coastal country of North Carolina, as in other sections throughout the United States) believe implicitly in the forked-limb method of locating water. It is called divining for water, and the forked limb, often from a peach tree, is known as a divining rod.

The man who uses this method in prospecting for water grasps the forked limb, securely but not with too strong a grip, in each hand, with the joint up, and walks along in the vicinity where the owner wishes to dig a well. When he gets over a stream or pond of underground water, the forked stick will twist in his hands until the joint points downward. The place where he is standing is marked, and there the well is dug. And invariably, say those who insist that this is an infallible method of locating water, an abundant supply will be found at that very spot.

"Many newspaper and magazine articles have been written about the divining-rod method of finding underground water and the amazing efficacy of the forked-limb prospector," Dr. Cannon comments. "And many explanations have been advanced. Some believe that the water diviner has an amazingly sensitive ear and that although he himself may not realize it he actually hears the moving underground water when he's above it. I very much doubt that, however. Others contend that it's a sort of sixth sense that enables him to do it and that the forked limb has nothing to do with it. The holder of the limb, they insist, himself turns the joint down, perhaps in obedience to the command of this sixth sense, psychologically. I surely have no explanation for it, and my attitude, I must confess, is one of profound skepticism. But the point I wish to make is that I would never tell any of my peach-tree-limb water prospectors or their customers that I doubted their ability to locate with their jointed limb a proper place to dig a well. No, never!"

But of all the strange superstitions that through the years have been given credence by many of the doctor's patients, the strangest, he thinks, is the one relating to an expectant mother and the imminent birth of her baby. He relates this incident:

"One day while I was away on a call a few months ago, a man brought his wife to our obstetrics clinic. The obstetrics patients were being cared for in the two-story cottage that had been provided by expanding the two-car garage that was there when I bought the property. Peggy Cowart was on duty when the man arrived with his wife, and it was immediately evident to her that the woman might give birth to her baby at any moment. One thing that we have not yet been able to teach our people is to arrange for expectant mothers to be examined and cared for during the prenatal period, and often I don't see a woman until an hour or so before the baby arrives."

Ordinarily in such cases, if it appears to the nurse on duty that labor pains may begin before the doctor can get back and it seems that there will be time to get the expectant mother to

To many patients who live in cabins hidden on steep mountain sides Doc Cannon's presence is as curative as the medicine he dispenses.

Over several hundred square miles of North Carolina's most inaccessible Blue Ridge coves and hills the name Doc Cannon is magic.

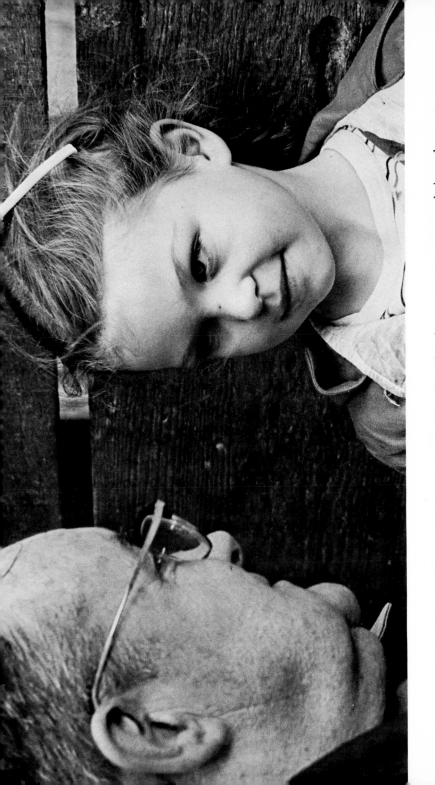

He's a big fellow, a year or two past sixty, but when he peers at you over steel-rimmed specs his grin is boyish.

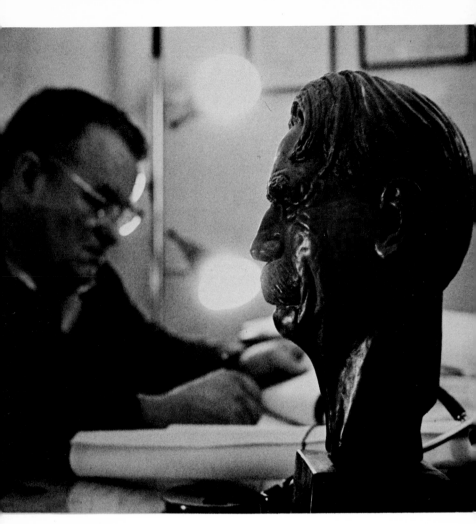

He tries to apply to his own situation Schweitzer's principle of reverence for life.

Helen McCall (center) is Doc Cannon's girl Friday. Nurse Gertrude Raschke worked with Albert Schweitzer for two years before coming to Balsam Grove.

It seems a long time ago that he first started to plan the Albert
Schweitzer Memorial Hospital with less than five dollars in the bank.

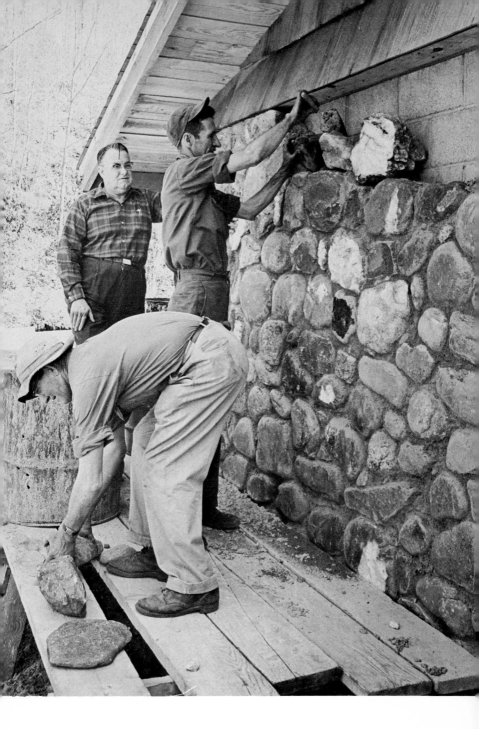

It was agreed that each patient coming to the clinic should bring two good, solid, rounded river stones on each visit to the doctor.

"I don't know anyplace in the world I'd rather be than right here among my own folk, where I can help people who but for me might not get help."

ALBERT SCHWEITZER MEMORIAL HOSPITAL

the Transylvania County Hospital, twenty miles away at Brevard, the nurse will start with her for the hospital rather than attempt to deliver the baby herself. But this day it was quite apparent to Peggy Cowart that there would hardly be time to make the trip to Brevard. So she helped the young woman into the little obstetrics cottage, and since she was the only person on duty at the time, began preparations for making the delivery.

"But hardly had she got the woman on the delivery table, which was a hospital bed equipped for that purpose, when the woman's husband came into the room. He was carrying a double-edged timberman's ax, and the edges of the ax had been sharpened to a fine gleaming. He started toward the bed on which his wife, already in the beginning travail of childbirth, lay moaning.

" 'I hope you don't mind,' he said to Peggy.

"Speechless, Peggy watched as the husband carefully placed the ax under the bed, directly beneath his moaning wife. Then he walked out of the room. In a few minutes Peggy delivered the woman successfully and with the help of one of the women employed there got the new mother back into the bed from which she had been brought into the delivery room. Whereupon the husband appeared a second time; he retrieved his ax from beneath the delivery bed, carried it into the other room, and placed it under the bed to which his wife had just been transferred."

When Dr. Cannon returned to the clinic, Peggy Cowart reported to him what had happened. She had made no comment to the young husband, she said, for fear it might provoke him to some desperate action.

"I just went along with the delivery and pretended not to notice that ax under the bed," she told the doctor.

Dr. Cannon laughed. He was familiar with this ax-under-the-bed practice. "That was an important obstetrical procedure that evidently they overlooked teaching you when you were taking your training, Peggy," he observed. "And it's one that you certainly should be familiar with." Then grinning, he proceeded to explain:

"The freshly sharpened two-edged ax with one edge cuts the pain and with the other keeps the patient from hemorrhaging. Both blades must be newly sharpened before the ax is put under the bed, and then nothing can be cut with it until after the baby is delivered and the mother has completely recovered from the delivery."

These are the ax-under-the-bed rules, and in the mountain communities those who follow such rules follow them explicitly, Gaine Cannon knows. "If, for instance, a person in sharpening an ax to be put under a delivery bed should accidentally cut his finger on it," he adds, "then he must start all over again and sharpen both its edges. And another thing I know," the doctor says emphatically. "I know that I would never even intimate to any of my mountain folk that I had the slightest doubt about the ability or the willingness of a properly sharpened two-edged ax to cut delivery pains or to prevent hemorrhaging, but I might suggest that a whiff of chloroform might *help* the ax in its functioning."

Some folk in the Blue Ridge and Great Smoky Mountains, where long-held traditions and beliefs still persist, likewise attach certain mystical powers to persons born out of wedlock.

Dr. Cannon tells the story recently related to him by a friend from the Piedmont section of the state who with several other friends was playing golf on a mountain resort course. This man had holed out on one green, and he and his caddy, a native of that section, were talking as they walked toward the next tee. The two had become quite chummy during the game, and the usual reserve of the mountaineer had begun to thaw. Up ahead another player and his caddy were leaving the tee that Dr. Cannon's friend was nearing. His caddy nodded his head toward the other one.

"See that caddy over there, mister?" he asked. "That fellow might come in mighty handy for you sometime."

"But you suit me fine," the golfer told him. "If I ever get back here to play, why couldn't I have you again?"

"Oh, I wasn't atalkin' 'bout playin' golf. I meant if you needed help if you got sick or hurt or somethin'. That fellow over there, he's got the gift."

"What do you mean, the gift?"

"He can cure you. If you get cut, he can stop the bleedin' by just atouchin' the cut place. Stuff like that. W'y, mister, if you should get api'soned by p'ison oak, he can cure it by just ablowin' on it; even if you got ap'isoned in the mouth, he could blow in your mouth and cure it right off like."

The downstate golfer was amused. "Well, how do you account for his being able to do that?" he asked.

"He was a base-born child."

"Base-born child? What do you mean?"

"His pappy and mammy wasn't married," the caddy explained.

With the approaching end of a century and a half of isolation in the North Carolina mountains, Gaine Cannon is afraid that soon a couple in a cabin at the crest of the Blue Ridge will hardly be distinguishable from a couple in a two-bedroom subdivision brick-veneered house in Charlotte or Greensboro or Raleigh.

But there is one aspect of life in the mountains, certainly in the large area he crosses daily in his faithful Renault, that is little changed in these modern days from the days of his boyhood, unless it has changed and is continuing to change for the worse.

"As a mountain doctor I am in a position to appreciate perhaps more than most of our citizens the tremendous and growing problem, I fear, of alcoholism," he declares. "In our immediate community—and that is the situation throughout the mountain area as well as the nation generally—we have many Vernons, both men and women."

Dr. Cannon believes that alcoholism is worse in the North Carolina mountain countries, which still forbid the legal sale of alcoholic beverages, than in those communities where the sale of such beverages is legalized and controlled. "I'm sure that this statement will be disputed by some of our preachers and ardent prohibitionists, but I do believe it is a fact. The preachers—and I hasten to admit that they sincerely believe they are right—have had more to do with keeping our mountains legally dry, though actually wet, than any other group of citizens. Paradoxically, while they are vehemently against the use and sale of liquor, by opposing the legalized sale and control of alcoholic beverages actually they align themselves with the moonshiners and the bootleggers who also oppose such controls.

"So most of the drinking in the mountains, often out of necessity as well as preference, has been confined to the consumption of corn whiskey. And corn whiskey is potent stuff. It will floor the man who has been a regular patron of the liquor stores."

In the course of his work Dr. Cannon has treated many habitual drunkards. He has taken some of them into his clinic, for he knew they did not have the money to pay for treatment in regular hospitals. "We do it, I suppose, because of our reverence for life," he says. "Often they are half starved and anemic, because when they go on extended sprees they have no appetite for food. All cases of alcoholism, of course, are pitiable, and many turn out tragically; but often some of these folk are delightfully amusing, too. Vernon, my Balsam Grove friend down the road, for example."

But although Dr. Cannon is an inveterate enemy of alcoholism, he fights it medically in furthering the realization of his philosophy of reverence for life, never as a citizen supporting the law-enforcement agencies. "They've had three stills on my property here that I know about," he reveals, "but I've never bothered them. You report one of these moonshiners and make him mad at you, and he might burn your house down. It has happened around here before, as it has happened throughout the moonshining areas in the mountains, and it could happen right here on the hospital property. Therefore I ignore any moonshining operations I find out about; I never report them to the revenue men or the sheriff's deputies, and so I remain their friend.

"Besides, I feel that it's none of my business. I'm not a law-enforcement officer. I don't preach morals to the folk around Balsam Grove, and I don't preach law observance. I'm their doctor. I do not report the presence in our community of fellows who have taken French leave of the various prisons and work-gang camps. If I inadvertently come upon such an escapee, I just fail to recognize him!"

"Dr. Cannon," Peggy Cowart explains, "simply sees everything through the eyes and with the feelings of the poor and the suffering, the underprivileged and the mistreated. He would laugh at the use of the word as applying to him, but he is one of the most *dedicated* persons I've ever known, a man with a great heart. He's a simple man with simple tastes, and his personal wants are easily satisfied. But his ambitions for the hospital and for bringing a better life to the people of the mountains are unbounded. And he is a good doctor; he is known in the profession as an unusually capable diagnostician. I'd say he was a perfect doctor to serve the mountain people with the facilities he has. And they will agree; they are confident that he's the best doctor in the world."

She speaks of an experience she shared with him in treating one of the community's unfortunates and describes it as illustrative of the doctor's quick sympathy generously expressed.

In 1958, Gaine Cannon converted a residence in Brevard into a clinic and began to divide his time between the Transylvania county seat and Balsam Grove. He customarily spent every Sunday and Wednesday at Balsam Grove and usually the other days he maintained his headquarters in Brevard.

"On his travels back and forth between Brevard and Balsam Grove, Dr. Cannon would stop at least once a week at the house of a friend who lived between Brevard and Rosman. This man had been an able worker, a pipe-fitter in one of the plants around Brevard, but because of his heavy drinking he had lost his job and become an alcoholic derelict. He lived by himself; he had lost his family, and for companionship had only two huge German shepherd dogs, who often slept in bed with him.

"One day on stopping at this man's shack Dr. Cannon found the door closed, and no one answered his knocking. But he could hear the dogs inside, and when he peered in a window he saw the man lying on the hearth, apparently dead.

"The dogs were ferocious, and more so that day because they were half starved. But by talking gently to them Dr.

Cannon at length cajoled them into letting him enter the house. He found the man badly burned but still alive, though unconscious. Evidently in a drunken stupor he had fallen on the hearth. One arm was terribly burned at the elbow; it appeared that the man had lain there with his elbow in the edge of the fire until the flames had burned out. The shack was then very cold (it was in February 1959), and Dr. Cannon was afraid that if the man could be restored to consciousness he would die of pneumonia. Later he discovered that his patient had been lying there about a week, burned and without food or water. The dogs had been able to knock some food from the decrepit kitchen table and had drunk from the water bucket as long as the water lasted. The odor in the closed-up shack was almost unbearable.

"But Dr. Cannon got the fellow bundled up and into his car, and brought him to Balsam Grove. Then he sent for me. It happened that I had not gone home to Florida, as I usually do in the fall, because I was up here supervising the building of our summer home. So I went over to the clinic, and immediately I knew that we had a tough job cut out for us if we were to save that fellow's life.

"Doc said that we'd have to operate. But we had no facilities for performing the kind of operation this fellow needed. I went upstairs in the old farmhouse-clinic and scrubbed one of the rooms. I scrubbed it all over—the walls, the floor, everything. Of course, I had moved the furniture out. Then I put newspapers on the scrubbed floor and laid freshly laundered sheets over the papers. I was determined to make that improvised operating room as sterile as possible.

"Then Dr. Cannon operated. And do you know, that fellow not only lived, but he regained most of the use of that arm. And the weather was so fearfully cold the rest of the winter that Doc kept him at Balsam Grove—in fact, he stayed for the summer. And we got him off liquor. Dr. Cannon told him that if he didn't stop he'd be dead. And not long afterward he did die, but not of alcoholism. He had an aneurysm, and of course, when the artery gave way he was gone. But Dr. Cannon had done all he could for the man, and without pay, except the pay that comes of doing a poor fellow a good turn."

CHAPTER
8

But of course not all the unique characters who came under Gaine Cannon's treatment are alcoholics or moonshiners. There is one man (the doctor calls him Frank, but that is not his name) who every few months, sometimes oftener, comes bursting into the doctor's office, whether Gaine Cannon at the time is seeing a patient or not.

"Doc, I ain't ajokin'," he'll declare excitedly. "By George, Doc, if you don't do somethin' for me, I'll be a dead man in fifteen minutes! I ain't ajokin', Doc; I'll shore be dead if you don't do somethin' for me right now. Now if you can't do nothin', Doc, just tell me and let me die, and call the undertaker. Now I mean it, Doc. I ain't ajokin' none. If you don't do nothin' right quick like, I'm a dead 'un."

If Dr. Cannon did nothing for him, he wouldn't die, certainly within fifteen minutes, Dr. Cannon knows. But the man does have pain, in the side of his head, he invariably tells the doctor, and at times it must be severe. So usually Dr. Cannon gives him several injections of a drug to relieve him and then after a while he will ask Frank if he isn't feeling better.

"Yeh, Doc, but mighty little," he will reply. "But, by George, if I wasn't afeelin' a little better, Doc, I'd already abeen dead."

"Though I believe some of his pain is psychological," Gaine Cannon says, "he must have something wrong in his spine that at times causes him to suffer acutely. Once I gave him some hypodermic injections and also some medicine to take home with him to use when the pain struck him. He went home and took all that medicine in one dose. They called me to rush out to his house, and when I got there he was in pretty bad shape; I thought for a while that despite everything I could do he was going to die. I gave him artifical respiration by breathing into his mouth, and before long we were able to get some firemen out from town with oxygen. I must have been giving him artificial respiration for two hours before they arrived with their equipment. Altogether I was with him more than six hours, and all that time my office was full of patients waiting for my return."

Cervical traction has been tried, but it has failed to help Frank. Dr. Cannon feels that there has been some deterioration of the vertebrae in the neck and that the new formation of bone structure is rough and at times presses against the nerves, causing intense pain. He has thought of having an operation performed on his patient, but feels that there has been too much deterioration, and he doubts whether Frank's condition is strong enough to carry him successfully through surgery.

'So about all we can do for Frank is relieve the pain when it gets intense," he confides. "When he comes storming in and shouting 'By George, Doc, if you don't do somethin' for me, I'll be dead in fifteen minutes! Just tell me if you can, and if you can't, just call an undertaker, by George, and I'll be dead 'fore he gets here!' then I start giving him injections—Sultein and Decadron and phenobarbital—and after a while I'll say, 'Well, Frank, you're feeling better, aren't you?'

" 'Well, maybe a little bit, Doc. But, by George, Doc, just a hair. No more'n a hair better.' "

Another patient Dr. Cannon treats regularly is a delightful old gentleman well past eighty. He has an especial liking for candy; he's a child that way. So after he has given him his treatment for the day, the doctor will reward him with candy.

"Doc, I don't mind takin' a shot so long's you give me some candy," he will declare happily. And one day when Dr. Cannon told the old fellow to take all the candy that was left in the box from which he had given him his allotment, he emptied the box into his pockets.

On another occasion Peggy Cowart, who had been in and out of the reception room while this old man was seated there with his wife as he waited to see the doctor, noticed him filling his pants pockets with candy from a box on the table nearby. His wife, too, saw him, and she began to reprimand him.

"Now you're just bein' childish," she scolded. "Don't you know he'll give you some candy?"

"Yes, I know that," her husband answered, grinning. "But he'll put it in my coat."

"Well, you know if you want candy all that bad, you can buy some," she persisted.

"I know that, too," he replied. "But over here I get it free just for takin' a shot. And I have to pay for the shot."

Another old man's taste appears to run to women. This patient is also past eighty. Dr. Cannon and the others about the hospital tease him about the girls, and he loves it. One day he was complaining mightily because the girl across the street from the house where he was living had exchanged her shorts for a skirt. At the time Peggy was preparing to give the old gentleman an injection.

"Where do you want me to give it to you?" she asked him.

"It just don't make no difference to me, honey," he replied, his old eyes bright, "just anywhere you can give it to me while you're asittin' on my lap."

One of the remarkable characteristics of the mountain folk, Dr. Cannon has discovered in his practice, is that many of them seem to maintain their sex interest and vigor into old age. As a physician he has unusual opportunity to observe some astonishing, if amusing, evidences. One day, for example, an old gentleman evidently in his eighties brought his wife, who was almost eighty, into the Balsam Grove clinic for an examination. Dr. Cannon gave her a very thorough examination, and as a result of his findings he suggested that it might be well for her to have her gall bladder removed.

The doctor's suggestion, however, was not received with enthusiasm, he noticed, but he presumed that the old lady was apprehensive that at her age a gall bladder operation might not go well. So he assured her that the risk would be small and gave her some medicine to calm her while she considered the proposal. But he was called out of the office, and it was not until after his patient had left that he learned from the nurse why the old lady had appeared worried after he had announced to her his diagnosis of her trouble and had recommended an operation.

"Paggy, Doc Cannon says I ought to let 'em take out my gall bladder," she had reported when the doctor left the room and Peggy Cowart came in. "But I don't know 'bout that, and I don't know what Daddy would say." 'Daddy' was her octogenarian husband. "And I was too shamefaced to ask the doctor," she confided, grinning, "but if they took out my gall bladder, I was just awonderin' if that'd change things 'tween me and Daddy. If it did change things that way, Paggy, I just know that'd make both of us mighty narvous."

The nurse, amused and also amazed, though she tried not to show it, assured the old lady that removal of her gall bladder would in no way change things for her. And thus assured, she readily agreed, when Dr. Cannon returned to the office, to have the operation. In fact, she was so relieved and happy that she called to her husband, waiting just outside the office:

"Now come on in, Daddy, and get your prassure took. You know you ain't been afeelin' so good lately."

But another patient, a mountain woman about eighty-five years old who had come down into the foothills for an operation at Baptist Hospital, at Winston-Salem, was not so reticent as the one who had brought her problem to Peggy Cowart. She questioned Dr. Cannon himself.

This old lady had developed an ulcer that had resulted in the removal of a part of the stomach. But the operation had been successful, and she went home to recuperate. As soon as she was able to get out she came to Dr. Cannon for a checkup to see if the wound was healing properly. The doctor examined her and found her making excellent progress toward recovery. He told her so.

The old soul was noticeably pleased. "That's good, Doctor," she said. "I'm mighty glad to hear it. But I wonder—it's kind of embarrassin' for me to ask you this, but you're supposed to be able to ask your doctor anything 'bout your health, they tell me, and—" She hesitated.

"Yes, ma'am," Dr. Cannon assured her, "that's right. You can ask me anything, and I'll tell you if I know the answer. Go right ahead."

[93]

"Well, Doctor, I've been home from the hospital now 'bout three weeks and you say I'm doin' all right. What I'd like to know now, when would it be all right for me to be a real wife to my husband again. You must know what I mean, don't you?"

Gaine Cannon knew what the old lady meant indeed, but he was amazed, as Peggy Cowart had been at the other patient's similar question. He answered casually, however, as though the question had not been an unusual one. "Let's see, you have been out of the hospital about three weeks, you say. I think it would be all right any time now."

The old woman smiled happily. "Thank you, Doctor," she said. "I was ahopin' that's what you'd say. And now, Doctor, don't you laugh at me"—she grinned—"but that makes me mighty anxious to be agettin' on home."

"Eighty-five years old! To me that is wonderful!" Dr. Cannon exclaims when he talks of the old lady and other cases. "It's a tremendous thing when couples that old can still love each other in a romantic way and be at least somewhat as they were when they were beginning their married lives and having their children. When I mention such cases to friends from other sections they are generally dumbfounded and say, 'But that must be highly unusual; it must be a case in a million, or at least a thousand!'

" 'No,' I say to them, 'the best thing about it is that it isn't tremendously unusual.' It is unusual, of course, and I can't deny that even though I'm very partisan in my descriptions of our mountain folk. Maybe I should say rather that it is unusual that we hear about such cases. I would never have heard of these two cases, for instance, if the old women hadn't been seeking professional advice, even though one of them was too shy to ask me directly. But this I can say positively—as positively as any physician can say as a result of examinations of and conversations with elderly patients, women and men— age seems to have little to do, in the cases of many of our mountain folk, with the retention or loss of their sex interest and vigor.

"A year or two ago a couple came up here from Florida to spend a short vacation in the mountains," Gaine Cannon further reports. "They were around forty years old, I suppose, and their youngest child was twelve. They went back home, and a month later I had a post card from the wife. It provoked considerable talk, because everybody at the post office read it, of course, and the story got around quickly.

" 'I'm going to have a baby,' said the message on the card. 'You'd better warn visitors about that mountain water up there.' "

"Well, we've laughed about that card," says Dr. Cannon, "but it really did set me to thinking. I wouldn't say it was the water, of course, though actually the pure water we have in the mountains, free of treatments they have to give it in municipal water systems, must contribute to the healthfulness of our mountain region.

"I believe this long-maintained vigor must be a result of our folks' living at a more relaxed tempo than the people of the big cities, as well as the fact that physical conditions are more healthful. I have been reading recently, for example, of the powerful effect upon the people of the smog in London and sometimes in Los Angeles and other great cities, and the always present gases from automobile exhausts. We have few if any such problems in the mountains, of course. But even more important, I believe, is this business of tempo. Our folk take it more leisurely; they believe in the slow and easy life. They are never, for long, at any rate, on a treadmill. They live more moderately. Take a city couple, for example, both working. They leave home early, and it's a continuous rushing for each all day long until they rush home, rush at preparing the evening meal, rush out to a meeting of some sort, whether it's a dance or a show or a parent-teacher meeting or any one of countless committee meetings, then rush home to take the baby sitter to her home, and rush to bed in order to get up in time to repeat the routine the next day. And there are countless other things to do that the mountain folk never have to do: driving the children to two or three different schools, picking them up again after school, driving them to the football field to practice or the school auditorium for band practice, or any number of other chores for the youngsters, not to count shopping, and going to the laundromat, the beauty shop, the airport. There's no end to the running about that must be done.

"But in the mountains folks don't burn themselves out that way. They don't gulp down their meals on the run. And after supper there are few meetings to go to. If a family has a television set, they sit around and watch it until eight or eight thirty and then they go to bed. They live at home. By now most mountain families have freezers, and they store their food and consequently are able to live at home. They cure their meat and put it up in the smokehouse, they can fruits and berries and vegetables, and oftentimes they dry fruit that in the winter makes mighty good pies, apple turnovers, and the like. They put chickens in the freezer and sometimes they can them; I've seen many a chicken put up in glass jars, along with beef and pork, cooked and sealed tight. So our folk don't have to be running around all the time. Maybe once a week a family will go to town in the pickup and get some salt and pepper and coffee and such staples, but they don't have to chase out to the supermarket every day or so. In fact, they don't rush about doing chores; they take their time. There is a quietness about their living that I don't believe you find as a general thing in the cities. And this, I suspect, is conducive to their having longer sex lives than the people in the more populated areas."

But frequently, Dr. Cannon adds, he will have a patient come to him seeking medical help in restoring sex vigor he fears has been lost or impaired. He tells of such a man who came one day to the clinic at Balsam Grove.

"Doctor, I'm a minister of the Gospel," the man introduced himself. Then he hesitated. "We're—we're human beings all alike, whether we're preachers or not. We all have our family duties to take care of, Doctor, and—and well, I'm sort of falling down on mine, and I've come to you for a little help."

"Preacher," Gaine Cannon said to him, "I've got some pills here that I've been prescribing, and my patients who have tried them tell me they're very good."

"I want the best thing you've got, Doctor," he said.

The doctor gave him thirty-six pills, along with instructions for taking them, and the preacher left. It was not until some six months later that Dr. Cannon saw him again, when one day he walked into the office.

"Doctor," he announced, "I'd like to get three more of those little black pills."

The doctor counted out the pills, and the preacher departed. But in two weeks he was back to ask for three more pills. And that routine continued for several months. "Doctor," he would say on each visit, "let me have three more of those little black devils."

One day as Dr. Cannon happened to be looking out through the office window, he saw the preacher coming, and he decided he would quiz him about the pills. "Preacher," he said when the man came in and gave his usual order, "do you mean to tell me that just three of those little pills are really helping you?"

"Good heavens, Doctor," the preacher exclaimed, "it just wouldn't do for me to get more than three of those little black devils at a time!"

News of the remarkable efficacy of the little black pills must have spread over the Balsam Grove community and into surrounding regions. On another day an old gentleman in that section who had lost his wife months before came to seek the doctor's help. His wife had been an invalid for a long time, and he had been good to her during all that trying period; she had finally died of cancer. Now he was free again, and beginning to look around.

"Doc," he said, "I been ahearin' tell that you got some black pills that's mighty good to help a fellow's manhood."

So Dr. Cannon told him that he had been prescribing the black-pill treatment for some of his patients and that they had been quite satisfied with the results.

"Well now, Doc," he said, nodding approvingly, "I want you to fix me up some of them pills."

Dr. Cannon counted him out a supply. Several weeks later on a visit to Brevard the doctor saw him. "Mr. Brown, how've you been making out with those pills I gave you?"

He beamed his delight at being questioned. "Doc, by George, I'm a new man," he declared. "Them little pills is the finest things ever I seen. I'm coming over to Balsam Grove pretty soon and I want you to give me another supply." A week or so later he came for them.

Then Dr. Cannon saw nothing of him for two months or longer. But one day he came to the office. "Doc, maybe you heared 'bout me gettin' married again?"

"Yes, Mr. Brown, I did hear something about that," the doctor replied.

"Well, I did. I married this woman, and that's how come I'm here. She's a good deal younger than me, and she's a big, strappin' woman, Doc. She ain't so tall, but she's wide, Doc; she must weigh more'n two hundred pounds." His face darkened with a troubled scowl. "Doc, look ahere, you're agoin' to have to do something for me. That woman—well now, Doc, I got to have help. I tell you, I just can't keep up with things the way it is now."

"Well, Mr. Brown, I've been giving you those little black pills, you know," the doctor said in confiding tone, "but here lately they've got out something that they tell me works better than those pills. I've been giving it in shots. I have an idea that is what you need." He told him about the new treatment and suggested that for a week or two he come to the clinic for an injection each day. "Then I'll begin giving you one every other day, and pretty soon maybe two a week, and then I'll cut them down to one a week, and before long to maybe two a month."

"Doc, that sounds mighty good," he replied, his relief evident. "But I want the best thing you've got, you can be sure of that."

So Gaine Cannon gave him an injection, and the next day he returned for another. He continued to come to the clinic in accordance with the schedule of treatments they had arranged, and the doctor had cut the treatments down to one or two a week when one day Dr. Cannon was looking out through the window of his private office and saw a woman coming toward the clinic building. She was very large; the doctor would have guessed she weighed not less than three hundred pounds. She was as wide as she was tall, and she waddled like a duck as she came determinedly along the walkway. In a moment he heard her come into the outer office. But she didn't stop to join the several patients who were waiting their turn with the doctor. She waddled right past them into Dr. Cannon's inner office, where he was engaged with a patient.

"Look ahere, Doc," she bellowed as she glared at him, hands on hips, "what kind o' shots have you been agivin' my old man?"

"Just some little tonic shots, Mrs. Brown," Dr. Cannon told her. "Just some shots to build him up."

"Well, look ahere, Doc," she thundered, "you stop it!"

And there in the presence of the patient on the examining table and in the hearing of everybody in the waiting room, she proceeded to tell him, in words plain and clearly understandable, why.

CHAPTER

9

GAINE CANNON is a modern physician in training and experience, but sometimes his practice routine is reminiscent of the horse-and-buggy doctor of two generations ago.

"Though I do attempt, in spite of the demanding duties I have, to keep abreast of the fast-moving advances in medical science in the treatments and the medicines I prescribe for my patients," the doctor says, "I am sometimes forced to employ techniques in treating them, and particularly in getting to their homes and occasionally taking them to hospitals at Brevard or Asheville or Greenville, that would make old Doc Adams of Gunsmoke in his horse and buggy look like a modern physician on his rounds."

This was especially true during the heavy snows in the early spring of 1960. Ordinarily the weather is very cold in the Balsam Grove region of the mountains during the winter months, but in March of that year the temperature dropped to record low readings. The snow drifts all but obliterated the twistings and turnings of innumerable trails leading to cabins that even in good weather often are inaccessible by automobile. For four weeks hundreds of families in the North Carolina mountains were snowbound. The weather over the nation, in fact, was bad. On the western plains feedstuffs were being flown to cattle marooned on snow-swept grazing ranges. And even in the North Carolina mountains planes were being used to fly in food and medicines, blankets and other supplies to homes cut off from contact even with their close neighbors.

During those weeks of ordeal few patients could get to Gaine Cannon's clinic, and he tried to go to them. He made calls all day long and often all night long, sometimes not getting to sleep until four or five o'clock in the morning and then resuming his calls again by seven. Time came to mean little, and he hardly knew the day of the week. Some mornings he would start out early with a list of fifteen or eighteen calls to make, most of the homes of patients miles apart, and he would treat others as he made his rounds. Other days he might start out at four o'clock in the afternoon and get back by daylight, if he was lucky.

Dr. Cannon was asked what would happen to him if on one of those bitterly cold nights he should be stranded. He wondered himself. But he always tried to start out prepared for almost any eventuality. He did not often go out alone. He wore heavy clothing, including insulated boots that worked somewhat like thermos bottles; if the wearer warmed his feet before putting on the boots, they would remain warm in spite of the cold and snow. Since the experience of the 1960 storm Dr. Cannon has kept a pair of the boots always available. "If I can keep my feet warm," he said, "I can usually get along without much trouble." During that rigorous winter he did get stuck in the snow occasionally, but he always managed to get out and keep going. He estimates that during those four weeks of heavy snows he made between four hundred and five hundred calls over his region of the mountains and treated persons for every sort of ailment.

"One day I received this urgent call to see an elderly woman who lived on Pinnacle Mountain, between Transylvania and Jackson counties," he recalls. "Aunt Carnettie Owen—her name was probably Carnetta, though everybody called her Aunt Carnettie—was then past seventy, and she lived alone. But some of her children visited her once or twice a week and carried her groceries; they had to walk the last few miles to get to her little cabin. One of them on such a visit had discovered her marooned in the deep snow and suffering with a huge leg ulcer; the poor old soul was sitting there crying in pain. So some of the children came over to see me about going up there to treat her. They had tried to bring her down, but she had refused to leave her little house.

"I agreed to attempt the trip but added that I would try to bring her down for more adequate treatment than I could provide in her hidden-away little cabin. Unfortunately, at that time my Jeep station wagon, which we called 'Old Faithful,' was in the shop having a new motor installed, the third one, if I remember correctly, and the only four-wheel-drive vehicle available was the Jeep pickup. So we loaded it with supplies and medicines, including a mattress and several heavy blankets, and started out. Six inches of fresh snow lay on the ground, and the only way up to Aunt Carnettie's place was little better than a cattle trail. Later we found out that there had been only one vehicle over that road ahead of us, a pickup truck that had been pulled by a team of horses."

Dr. Cannon took a Balsam Grove friend and two of the old lady's sons with him. The four men had a difficult time going up. The hardest problem was ascertaining where the trail was beneath that heavy covering of snow. It would have been hard enough to stay on it and move along even had they been able to see where they were going. In some places the road crawled around precipitous shelves on the mountainside; the shoulders were narrow and soft and the drifting snow effectively concealed the rounded edges from which the suddenly lurching pickup might tumble downward hundreds of feet.

"But Providence must have guided my driving," the doctor says, "for although we got stuck several times and had to push the Jeep out and other times narrowly missed rolling off the tortuous road, we finally reached the old lady's house. Cold! The cabin was on the top of a mountain in a small clearing across which the wind was whipping, it seemed to me, a hundred miles an hour. It felt like that wind literally would cut you in two.

"We maneuvered the vehicle as close to the house as we could get it. When we cut the motor, we could hear the poor old woman crying out with pain. We went inside and found a tiny fire going; her children had left some firewood in the house, and fortunately, she had been able to keep from freezing.

" 'You ain't agoin' to take me down there and cut my leg off!' she screamed when she saw me. 'You ain't agoin' to cut it off!'

"I hadn't said anything, of course, about cutting her leg off. In fact, I hadn't even had time to speak. But I attempted to reassure her immediately. 'Aunt Carnettie,' I said, 'nobody's even thinking about cutting your leg off.'

" 'Yes, you were, too!' she insisted. 'You were afixin' to take me down there and cut my leg off, and I ain't agoin' to let you do it. I ain't agoin' to have my leg cut off, I ain't!' The old lady was hysterical with pain and fear."

But Dr. Cannon succeeded in calming her after a while, and then he began to examine her leg. It was a fearful sight. She was a big woman and had large, unshapely calves. The ulcer, the doctor found, had eaten away in the calf until it was as big as a man's hand and almost down to the bone. He knew that it was frightfully painful, and he knew also that it would take long and careful treatment to induce the leg's healing. She could very well lose the leg because of it.

"Aunt Carnettie," he said to her after he had given the leg a cursory examination, "you knew my father, Dr. J. A. Cannon, didn't you?"

"Yes, o' course I did," she replied. "And he was a fine man, too, and if he was here right now he wouldn't be awantin' to cut my leg off, neither."

"Well, all I'm going to ask you, Aunt Carnettie," Gaine Cannon went on, "is to trust me and have the same confidence in me that you had in my father." He looked her straight in the eyes. "If I promise you something, I'll keep my promise; you can depend on that. Now, we may take you down the mountain and we may decide that it will be best to take your leg off. But I promise you that we won't do it unless you want it done. And the way it looks to me right now, Aunt Carnettie, I don't think it should be taken off. I think we can treat it and cure it, though it will take a little time."

He talked gently and reassuringly to her and got her quieted, and she agreed to let them take her down to Balsam Grove. They wrapped her in blankets and carried her out to the pickup, placed her on the mattress and covered her with more blankets, and then they started down the mountain, retracing the perilous miles they had come. Now they had one more life to safeguard. To add to the peril, it started snowing again as they began the descent. So as they slipped and twisted their way downward, they had to stop every mile or so to shake the snow from the blankets covering the patient. Finally they turned into the little road leading to the clinic, and for the first time since they had driven out hours earlier they were able to relax a bit.

That ulcer required long and careful treatment, as Dr. Cannon had thought it would. The infection was deep and stubborn. Flies, dust and dirt had aggravated the malady, and circulation of blood around the sore had almost stopped. It was a serious situation, and for a while the doctor wondered if after all the leg wouldn't have to be amputated in order to save her life. First he worked to get the circulation restored, and then at last he succeeded in getting the ulcer to bleed. The urgent need was to get the blood into it and the infection out.

He kept the patient at Balsam Grove while he built her up for the operation he knew would have to be performed. He realized that her folk would not be able to pay for a long stay in another hospital, and he was certain also that he could do as much for her at Balsam Grove—at very little cost, up to the point of surgery—as could be done for her anywhere else. She had varicose veins and had been on her feet much of the time, Dr. Cannon concluded. Doubtless she had scratched her leg with soiled fingernails. It had become infected, and the doctor knew that a long period of rest and treatment would be required to get her in condition for further treatment on the ulcer. So he kept her at the clinic and worked with her. Then one day Dr. Cannon carried Aunt Carnettie down to the Pickens hospital.

There was an excellent surgeon there, Dr. Cannon knew, for he was one of the doctors Cannon had brought to the Pickens hospital while he was operating it, before he moved up to Balsam Grove. "He and I put Aunt Carnettie to sleep, and we went after that ulcer." He recalls that "We scraped it out with something like a wire brush until we were down to good tissue and it was bleeding freely. Then we went up to her thigh and removed a patch of skin with which we covered the place where the ulcer had been.

"Eventually it filled out and healed completely. And although there's a depression in her calf where the ulcer was, the leg is in good shape. Aunt Carnettie is one of my staunch friends. Every now and then I see her and we laugh about the time she was so sure I was going to put her to sleep and cut off her leg, or worse, as she thought I might, have somebody hold her down while I cut it off, without anesthetics!"

It was during that big snow in March of 1960 that one day Gaine Cannon had a call from the sheriff's office and also from the state highway patrol, telling him that over in Jackson County there were some persons very ill and in desperate need of help. Would he make an effort to get to them?

Fortunately, the Jeep station wagon, its new motor installed, was back from the repair shop, and it was equipped with four-wheel drive and snow tires. It would go where nothing else on wheels would.

Dr. Cannon told them he would try to reach those people, but explained that before he could start out he would have to make about a dozen other calls. It was already afternoon. He would make a circle around by Owens Mountain and back over Nellie Mountain, and eventually get into the Pinhook community. The officers assured Dr. Cannon that they would send a bulldozer ahead to push the snow off the road so that he could get over it.

About four o'clock the doctor started. He took one of the hospital's trustees in case he fell asleep while driving. Recently he had been so tired that while alone he had been unable to drive safely. However, on this afternoon his friend not only kept him awake but also helped with the driving.

Doc Cannon completed the dozen calls up through the Lake Toxaway community and over across Owens Mountain along one of the worst roads in the region, and on over Nellie Mountain. The bulldozer had gone on ahead, but it was snowing and the going was still rough. But with the snow tires and all four wheels pulling, they finally made it. The doctor was able to treat quite a number of sick persons around Pinhook. Before leaving they had loaded the station wagon with food as well as medicines, because they knew that many of these people were snowbound and would be almost famished.

One of them was an old man named Charlie McCall, who lived a few miles behind Pinhook Gap. When they reached Charlie McCall's, they found a group there; the news had got around somehow that Dr. Cannon was coming to Charlie's, and these folk had assembled so that he could give them needed medical attention.

Gaine Cannon continues the story:

"I found Charlie, who was about seventy-five, sitting up in bed with a splint-bottom chair padded with pillows at his back. There was a puny fire smoldering in the fireplace, but because he was struggling to get his breath they had left the front door of his cabin wide open, and outside the temperature must have been down to zero. Four or five chunks of wood lay beside the fireplace, and there was hardly anything to eat in the house. Old Charlie was out of wood, out of food, out of medicine. He had pneumonia, he had a bad heart, kidney trouble, and about everything else that can go wrong with a fellow that old.

"Fortunately, I had a pretty complete pharmacy with me; on these trips I had to carry one because I never knew what sort of ailment or injury I might find and I knew that my patients wouldn't be able to get out or send to a drugstore to have prescriptions filled. So I gave Charlie some shots, and I arranged with the neighbors to have someone stay with him awhile and give him medicine I was leaving. And I laid in a stock of food for him. I instructed them to be sure to see that a fire was kept going, and that he took his medicine when he was supposed to. Then after I had treated the others who had come to see me, we stepped out into that bone-chilling air and started for home. On the way down the mountain behind that bulldozer that had been pushing the snow to the sides of the road, we drove through a cut with the snow on each side as high as our heads. But we got back to Balsam Grove without any unusual trouble."

Old Charlie pulled through. And he is still going strong, the doctor reports, despite the bad heart and bad kidneys and other ailments. Several months after Gaine Cannon's visit to him during the heavy snows he was again desperately ill; the doctor had to take him down from his cabin on a mattress. He had called an ambulance to meet them down on the highway and take him on to an Asheville hospital. Dr. Cannon thought then that he would surely die, but Charlie came out of that close brush with death, too, and before long was back home. "And the last news I had about him," the doctor says, "was that he was as pert as a cricket."

One of Dr. Cannon's most troublesome problems during those long days and nights of the great snow was delivering babies. "The baby crop in the mountains, as in all other regions, never fails," he says, "nor do the babies delay their arrival until the snows melt. I don't know how many babies

I did deliver during that four-week period; looking back, I seem to remember that the rate was higher than usual, though it probably wasn't. Perhaps it was just that the circumstances under which I made the deliveries were so much more trying than usual makes the number seem larger. And also I had to go out and bring many of these expectant mothers to our clinic."

If he can possibly avoid doing so, Gaine Cannon does not deliver babies in the homes. In the earlier years of his practice he did most of his delivering there, but for the last several years he has been trying to get the expectant mothers to come into the clinic. It is better for the doctor and to the patients' own advantage. The facilities in most homes are woefully inadequate, his back still troubles him, and it is particularly difficult for him to stoop over the bed in a mountain home.

But during that period of heavy snows many of the women expecting babies were unable to get to the clinic at Balsam Grove; an automobile, if the family had one, could not get through. So frequently Dr. Cannon had to take the Jeep station wagon and bring these women down to the obstetrics clinic. There he had a bed that he could raise or lower, and he delivered them on this bed. Though the clinic was equipped also with a regular delivery table, he more often used the bed. As Cannon explains, "It saves putting the patient on a stretcher and taking her into the delivery room and transferring her to the delivery table, and then after the delivery putting her back on the stretcher and rolling her out." He continues that procedure. If another woman is waiting for delivery, the attendants put the one who has just been delivered into another bed and prepare the first bed for the next delivery. And even in his small clinic often women are waiting. One day recently they had to move a newly delivered young mother out into the waiting room and place her on a daybed. Sometimes, too, though they have several in the obstetrics clinic, all the bassinets may be filled; but usually there are not more than two new babies there at the same time. And though because of this there is little danger of getting babies mixed, they always take the precaution of putting the babies' names both on their bassinets and on the bracelets on their wrists.

During that heavy snow the new mothers and their babies, snowbound away from their homes, remained in Gaine Cannon's obstetrics clinic for days, in some cases weeks. This was for longer than they would have stayed had the weather been normal. Usually the mountain woman, after she has had her baby, insists on going home almost immediately, often on the day of the baby's arrival.

"They don't want to linger," Dr. Cannon reveals. "As I have said, they are usually late getting to us. I think sometimes that they must wait down at our road entrance on the highway until the last minute before coming in to the clinic. I try to keep them at least one night following the delivery, but often they won't stay, especially if the babies are born in the morning. The North Carolina state law provides that an expectant mother must have blood tests during her pregnancy, but if they don't come in, then of course we can't give them the tests, and I note on her record that the patient didn't come in until labor had begun. These mountain women are little concerned about what these state laws require; all they want is to have their babies and get home. If a woman is having her first baby, I insist that she stay at least two nights, especially if she doesn't get along very well. I do the same way in the case of a woman who has had one or more babies if she's an RH negative, for instance, because I wish to observe such a case for a few days before sending her home.

"But most of the mothers seem to have an aversion to being away from home when night comes. Recently a young woman who had come in quite early had her baby about eight o'clock that morning.

" 'Doctor,' she asked me a moment after the baby's arrival, 'can't I go home this afternoon?'

" 'Well, if you continue to do all right,' I answered, 'maybe you can go home late this afternoon.'

"I had to go on a call that kept me away until the middle of the afternoon. When I returned I inquired about my OB patient.

" 'She left before lunch time,' the nurse reported.

"Another young woman not so long ago got up from her bed, bundled up her new baby, walked out to her car, a Jeep station wagon—which is a pretty rough-riding vehicle—and drove home the same day the baby was born."

He can tell them that it is most important that they stay at the obstetrics clinic a few days, but unless they are feeling ill most of them simply won't do it. Nor can the nurses or the doctor himself keep the mothers in bed while they're at the clinic. Peggy Cowart tells an amusing story that illustrates not only how quickly mountain mothers go home after the deliveries but also with what ease and dispatch many of them give birth to their offspring:

"Dr. Cannon wasn't at Balsam Grove when this woman came to the clinic; he was in a hospital himself, in Greenville, South Carolina. And there was no other doctor available. I was the only person there who had had any medical or nursing training and experience. Usually when a woman comes in to have a baby and the doctor is away, I either get another doctor or send her to the hospital at Brevard.

"But I saw at once that there wasn't time to attempt the

twenty-mile trip to Brevard. The woman was already well along in labor when she came in. I knew I'd have to deliver her. Several times before we'd had similar situations and I'd got along all right. But it's always a disturbing experience. This was an emergency though, and I'd have to take charge.

"I determined that the woman should have an enema and gave her one. And in another few minutes I delivered the baby, which I learned was her ninth child, and got her comfortably settled with a dip of snuff and a paper cup to spit in. Then I went into the bathroom to wash my hands and discovered that the woman had not flushed the toilet. I thought, of course, that she had failed in the excitement of expecting the baby to flush it. I flushed it and said nothing of it to her. But a little while afterward the woman got out of bed and went into the bathroom, and when she returned her amazement was evident. She had never seen a flush toilet before!

"I showed her how to flush it, and she watched with childish excitement as the water whirled about the bowl and disappeared from it. She was intrigued, and from then on every time she wanted to spit out her snuff she would climb out of bed, though she had just been delivered of a baby, and go into the bathroom, spit into the bowl, and flush it. 'I got a picture o' one o' them things at home in a catalogue,' she confided to me, 'but this is the first time I ever seen one.' She was as thrilled as a child with a new toy. It was impossible to keep her in bed even while she was recuperating from her delivery. That afternoon she went home."

This woman may have been the only patient past forty who had never been in a modern bathroom, but she was not unique in getting out of bed minutes after the birth of her baby or in going home the day it was born. "You can tell them not to get up for a while," Peggy says, "but few of them will pay any attention to your orders. Several times I have been in the back, cleaning up the new baby, and I'd hear a noise and it would be the mother trudging to the bathroom."

Although Dr. Cannon has delivered many babies in his clinic at Balsam Grove and throughout the extensive region he serves, often under unusual and challenging circumstances, he considers the most dramatic delivery he ever did was during that same heavy snow of 1960. He describes it as "bizarre even for my often somewhat unorthodox ways of practicing medicine." And he delivered the baby while he was engaged with a patient in another of his most unusual cases.

"I'd had this call from away over in Jackson County," he recounts. "An elderly woman was desperately ill. Could I possibly come? I told them I'd try.

"So I started out, and I did all right until I got up into Jackson County, and then I had to turn off the road and get up to the house where this old woman lived, away back up on the side of a mountain. There I was forced to stop; I just couldn't make it in spite of my chains and tires and four-wheel drive. But after a while a man came down from the house with a horse pulling a sledlike contraption with runners hewed out of small trees and turned up at the ends, and a little platform on it. It was rough going for the horse to get back up the hill, but we reached it, and I proceeded to examine the old woman. I discovered that she was ill of what is commonly called double pneumonia."

Dr. Cannon felt that it was impossible to get her to the hospital for treatment. So he gave her some injections and managed to get some medicine into her, and left instructions for caring for her until he could return. Then, he told them, he would try to take her to the hospital.

"Several days later I managed to get back to see her," he

says, "although once again it was a struggle. It had continued to snow. The last half mile up to her house took an hour's hard work. All that distance I was running forward a few feet to break a track into the snow, then backing up and running forward again to break the track a little farther. When I did get to the house, I started preparing the old woman for the trip down to the hospital. I was interrupted, however, when her son, who was old and alcoholic and had been making and drinking moonshine whiskey all his life, suddenly began having a severe hemorrhage. He was spitting up mouthful after mouthful of blood. My nurse, who had come along to help me with the old lady, was almost frightened out of her wits."

So Dr. Cannon had to stop to work on the old man. He gave him some hemostatic injections to stop the bleeding and penicillin and streptomycin to clear up the infection. The hemorrhaging, despite the nurse's alarm, appeared not to disturb him very much; he told them that he had bled like that a number of times before. And soon after the doctor finished treating him, the man was outdoors in all that snow, looking after his horse. He was paying little attention to what apparently was to him a small thing, and was walking about the barnyard, spitting blood into the snow.

"Well, I got the old lady into the station wagon," the doctor continues. "I had brought along a mattress and blankets and quilts, and several hot water bottles, and had managed to get the vehicle right up to her door, so that we had only a few steps to carry her before laying her on the mattress. We got down to the road without great difficulty, and started for the hospital at Brevard.

"Meanwhile (this I would learn later) a man and his pregnant wife had started for Balsam Grove to have me deliver her baby. They were walking, plodding slowly through the deep snow, and already the woman was in the first stages of labor, and they were over in Jackson County, fifteen miles from our clinic!

"Somewhere along the way—the woman's pains were getting closer together—the two came upon a station wagon parked on the side of the road. Fortunately, the keys were in the ignition switch. Without saying anything to the owner they climbed in and took off through the snow, heading for our clinic. But when they got here, I was still away on the old woman's case. They couldn't call me from Balsam Grove because I had no radio in my station wagon; I keep the two-way radio in my little Renault. So two of the nurses jumped into the station wagon that the couple had commandeered and headed with the man and his wife as fast as they could toward the hospital at Brevard.

"Just as they came out to the highway from the hospital grounds, they saw me go past in the Jeep station wagon with the old lady. They started after me as fast as their station wagon could make it through the snow, and soon came up behind me and began blowing their horn furiously.

" 'What sort of fools are those people, trying to race me in this snow?' I said to myself as I pulled over to the side of the road to let them go past. But the other station wagon stopped too, and I recognized my nurses in it. They quickly told me what the situation was. And fortunately, they had had the foresight to bring along an OB pack.

"I took one look at the woman and I knew there was no time to waste. The station wagon had three seats, and the woman was crouched down on the rear one; her husband was driving. I climbed quickly into the middle seat with one of the nurses, and had to lean over the back of the seat to deliver the baby. But I didn't have much to do. A moment after I'd got my rubber gloves on and turned to her the baby's lusty squalling shattered the peace of the snowbound landscape, and in the same instant a steady little stream arched out and downward from the new arrival.

" 'Look, Fred! Fred!' shouted the mother, apparently fully cognizant of as well as interested in everything going on. 'It's a boy!'

" 'Yeh,' observed the father imperturbably, 'I see it is.' "

In a few minutes Dr. Cannon's chore on the roadside was completed and he went on with the old lady to the hospital in Brevard, and the others turned around and drove back to the clinic. Soon after their arrival there, the man whose station wagon the couple had borrowed without leave came over to Balsam Grove. Someone who had seen the man and woman get into it had noticed that the woman appeared to be in the last stages of pregnancy and had suggested that perhaps the couple had headed toward Dr. Cannon's place. When upon coming to the clinic the owner learned what had happened, he was gracious about it.

The nurses had put the new mother to bed as soon as they got her to the clinic. Dr. Cannon arrived in the afternoon, and the woman and her husband immediately announced to him that they were leaving as soon as their transportation home arrived.

"But you can't go," the doctor told the mother. "You'll never get over the roads. It has snowed some more since you came in."

"Oh, yeh, we can," the man insisted. "We got a Jeep station wagon acomin' for us, with four-wheel drive and chains, just like yourn."

And when that station wagon did come for them Dr. Cannon let them go.

CHAPTER

10

Looking back to those bitterly cold weeks early in 1960, when deep snows all but obliterated twisting dirt roads hardly traversable by automobile in good weather and added immeasurably to the burdens and perils of a mountain doctor, Gaine Cannon wonders how he managed to retain his health, avoid accidents, and treat so many patients, some of them critically ill.

Reverence for life had much to do with it, he is convinced —his own, his associates', and his patients', particularly his patients'. "Every living creature has a will to live," the doctor maintains. "No creature wills to die—except man, and I believe that no sane man ever commits or seriously contemplates suicide. Every living thing that has a mind, however simple, runs from death, tries desperately to avoid dying. It may be only what we call instinct that impels him, but there's a will to live."

Dr. Cannon feels, too, that danger and struggle increase a creature's natural will to live, to persist. It may be, he suggests, that strong-willed persons in times of stress become all the more determined to defeat the enemies that would take them off, that would rob them of their identities, their existence. It may be—it must be, he thinks—that in times of peril people gain strength, whether one terms it mental, psychological, or spiritual; he believes these increased resources in turn provide added physical stamina. "I call this reverence for life," he says, "the will to live and to let live." But he goes further with his definition: "the will to live and to *help* other life to live." Not only his people, his beloved folk of the mountains, but people everywhere, of every race, color, clime; the privileged, the abandoned, the good, the bad. And not only all people, but animals, birds, fish, insects—*all* life, every creature that has the will to live. "Seeing any unnecessary dying, Dr. Schweitzer himself dies a little." And so does Gaine Cannon.

In those weeks of the great snow, too, there was no respite.

"I remember the first night the big snow came," he reminisces, "I was out making calls in my little Renault over on Frozen Creek Road, in the old Toxaway area, a very poor road in any weather. I hadn't even thought of snow. It was late on a Friday, and as we came out of the patient's house—Frank McCall, Helen's husband, was with me—we discovered that it had been snowing while we were inside; already, we were afraid, driving back would be hazardous. But we started, and every now and then Frank would have to get out and push, and by backing up and running forward, and backing again and running again, we finally got out on the highway; we drove on to Brevard, where I had left my Jeep. On the way back to Balsam Grove we thought several times that the Jeep wouldn't be able to make it through that snow over the bad roads we would have to travel. After struggling along, however, we did get home, and started getting the Jeep station wagon ready by putting four snow chains on it. With it we were able to make calls; we discovered that it would go where none of the others would. In fact, we often passed trucks and Jeeps abandoned by the roadside after they had been stuck in ditches and unsuspected snowdrifts. The station wagon has a longer wheel base and it's heavier and has larger, broader tires; I think that is the reason it is such a good snow vehicle. But even with it I sometimes got stuck. Four times I had to have a wrecker pull me in. I'd get in places where I couldn't tell where the road was, and get high-centered, so that soon all four wheels would be spinning."

Oftentimes in those weeks of fearsome weather he wondered if he would make it to some house high up on a mountainside, or get home again after having battled his way up there. Residents of the community would wonder too. Sometimes a group, gathered beside a road over which he was shoving his way through the snow, would shake their heads. "Nobody's been over this road today," one would declare soberly. "He'll never make it; he won't be able to get up there this time."

But the doctor always did. "I don't recall failing to get to a single case where I was desperately needed," he says. "The folk would stand along the roadside, the snow still unbroken, and watch. I suppose I was a sort of show for them."

During that month Dr. Cannon had some patients who were critically ill, and several died. But he doesn't believe he lost a single case because he was unable to get to the patient. Some days during those four weeks there would be neither a car nor a truck coming along the road leading from the highway to the clinic. But he always managed somehow to get through. He put chains on his little Renault and sailed along when the big cars were sticking everywhere. The snow would freeze on top, and his car was so light that it would skim along on the surface, but the big cars would break through and sit there spinning their wheels.

There were a few places that he never did reach with anything on wheels, despite four-wheel drives and snow chains. He isn't able to drive all the way into those homes even in good weather; actually there is no road to them, and the only way to get in is to ride horseback or walk. He wonders how people living in such places ever managed to build houses there.

"I particularly remember one such home, if one can call it a home," Dr. Cannon says. "I drove as far as I could toward it, and then got out and walked, lugging my heavy bag of medicines and supplies and instruments, down a steep hill, across a footlog and up another hill. Squatting in a little cleared space was a shack, crude even for the mountains, and inside I found a woman and five or six dirty, half-starved children. Her husband had run off to Florida, leaving her without a stick of firewood and hardly a bite to eat in the house. I had brought some groceries, and I trudged back to the car and got a supply that I left with her. The welfare people hadn't got around to helping her; I wondered if they'd even learned about her situation or how to get back in there to visit her."

Recalling trips like that one, Dr. Cannon wonders how many such homes he did visit during that four-week siege of deep snows. "I distinctly remember a place over in Jackson County that one of my nurses and I visited. I usually took a nurse, oftentimes Helen McCall, along when I gave out groceries because the nurse knew better than I did how to manage the situation, particularly when women and children were involved, and almost invariably they were. In this shack we discovered eleven persons living in three rooms. And filthy! I'm sure you could have scraped dirt off the floor with a garden hoe. One room had only a dirt floor. We had to walk to this house, too; the road played out completely before we reached the house. We went inside and set the groceries on the table. As we put the bag down, one of the children, a skinny, anemic youngster, reached up for a banana. The father, a hulking, animal-like fellow, slapped the child on the hand and grabbed the banana, which he proceeded to devour.

"I don't know when I've been angrier. But I didn't hit him, or even say anything, although I could hardly restrain myself. I simply reached over, picked up a banana, and handed it to the famished youngster. The father didn't say anything; he just stepped back and watched the child gulp the banana."

Dr. Cannon believes that the food he carried to families back in the hills and coves often did them as much good as the medicines he administered. In fact, some families told him later that the food he brought kept them from starving.

"But I don't take all the credit for supplying that food," he hastens to point out. "Others contributed. A lady in Brevard, for example, gave me some money with which to buy groceries for needy folk. 'You just take this money, Doctor,' she said, 'and buy what you think they should have. You know more about that than I do.'

"I'd usually take a basket that cost around ten dollars to a family; the size depended, of course, on the size of the family. It would be filled with staples, such as black-eyed peas, cabbage, potatoes, bread, sugar, coffee, a lot of canned things, bacon, maybe some jellies, things like that, plain but substantial food.

"But the help these families receive hasn't been limited to the weeks they were snowbound. Some of our people have a tough time of it during good weather, too, and I try to help them whenever their need is urgent. I have never become thin-skinned enough to look on complacently when little children, especially, are hungry. Many folk in our section are poor; some families make less than three hundred dollars a year; so they have a very poor diet, with usually but two or three kinds of food on the table day in and day out, and often too much hog fat."

He tells of having talked about this poor diet of many mountain families with Dr. Schweitzer when he was visiting the Schweitzer Hospital at Lambaréné. "Oh, no, no!" Dr. Schweitzer exclaimed. "*Das kann nicht sein!* That cannot be in a rich country like America!"

"But not all communities in America are rich," he said to Dr. Schweitzer, "and ours is one that isn't. We do have some fairly affluent families, though affluence is very much a matter of definition. What would be considered affluence in Transylvania and Jackson counties in the mountains surely would not be affluence in the metropolitan counties of North Carolina and the rest of the nation. In our immediate vicinity there are a few persons who consider themselves affluent. For example, such a person is the woman who has a job that pays her forty-five or fifty dollars a week. She drives out and back every working day, and she carries with her four or five other workers who pay her nominal amounts for their transportation; they ride in a station wagon that she has bought on credit and for which she is paying so much a month. She is managing to meet these payments, and is getting along very well. This woman—and there may be three hundred persons in our county in corresponding situations—considers herself quite affluent; she probably feels she's another Rockefeller."

Dr. Cannon estimates that the average income of the

Transylvania County worker is about twelve hundred dollars a year. The family then that has two or three persons working can get along very well, but a man with a wife and several children and only his own wages is hard pressed to make a living. Were it not for the fact that they have the Ecusta plant at Brevard, which, Dr. Cannon understands, makes more than one half of all the cigarette paper used in the manufacturing of American cigarettes, economic conditions in the region would be considerably worse. The average wage in that plant, he estimates, is between sixty and seventy dollars a week.

"Some of our people don't like these statistics to be spread about the country, as I was to learn one night during a meeting at the schoolhouse," he reveals. "We had put out a sixteen-page booklet, composed mostly of pictures of unique characters in our community, along with a short article describing them and the region, an article that was correct both in fact and interpretation.

" 'Balsam Grove is a typical community in the Blue Ridge Mountains of North Carolina,' this booklet began. 'It is covered with pine, oak, balsam, wild azaleas, mountain laurel, and rhododendron and cooled by fresh-water streams.

" 'The people are friendly but poor. Most of them are farmers who own a few acres or more, on which they raise pigs and cattle, produce their own canned and pickled goods, cut wood pulp, gather moss for sale to funeral parlors, and of course, make "corn," better known outside mountain country as "moonshine." '

" 'These people are largely isolated from the modern world. They often refuse to leave home to find work; some incomes are as low as three hundred dollars a year. Some families even refuse to send their children to school; consequently, much of the population is illiterate.' "

It was this last paragraph to which some of the folk at the schoolhouse that night objected, as well as to a later assertion by Dr. Cannon that many of the mountain folk did not have proper diets, a condition that made them subject to various ailments.

"How do you know this, Dr. Cannon?" one woman challenged. "How do you know that these people don't have the right kind of diet? You are low-rating our community; you're hurting us by this little booklet."

"In the end it never hurts to tell the truth," Dr. Cannon responded. "And you ask how I know these things, how I know about the diets of so many of our families. This is how I know. I doctor these people. I go into their homes, and I sit down at their tables and eat with them. I know what they have to eat, and what they don't have. Do you? Some of you people here tonight won't condescend to sit down and eat with some of these folk. But I eat with them. I know these people, and I want to help them. That's why we put out this booklet, to help create a wider interest in the hospital so that we can expand our services to them. And we can back up any statement in it. I surely know about their diet. I eat with them."

One of the Balsam Grove characters mentioned in the booklet is "Aunt Mary" McCall. Dr. Cannon thinks she is the oldest person living in the Balsam Grove community and certainly one of the oldest in Transylvania and Jackson counties. She is said to be a year or two past the century mark; he thinks she may be older.

"Aunt Mary was one of my father's patients, and now she's one of mine. She believes that we two have been the only really competent physicians in our times, and between the two of us I'm quite sure that she rates my father first. For his opportunities and times I, too, would give him the top rating.

"I have been treating Aunt Mary, who is troubled with arthritis and sometimes other ailments related more particularly to old age, for a long time, and she talks freely with me. She is an appreciative old soul, and philosophical. She talks intelligently, too, though I suspect that she is competely illiterate. Recently I was up to visit her; she was quite ill with acute chronic bronchitis. But she shook hands with me and told me how glad she was to see me. When I asked how she was feeling, she replied with complete frankness.

" 'Purty po'ly, Doctor,' she said. 'Purty po'ly. I just don't know why the good Lord is akeepin' me around; I just don't know why He's akeepin' me here.'

" 'Well, Aunt Mary,' I said, 'He must have a good reason or He wouldn't be keeping you. He must have a purpose. And I know all the people in the community love you and they want you to stay around as long as you can.'

" 'I know they do, too,' she said, smiling. 'And I'm glad they do, but it does seem just kind of useless. I ain't no good no more to nobody.' "

Mrs. McCall has children who are seventy-five or eighty years old, perhaps older, and quite a number of great-great-grandchildren. One of her sons, well past seventy-five, operates a little grocery store near Brevard and at least once each week he carries a supply of groceries to his mother.

The noteworthy thing about the old lady, however, is not her great age, though having passed the century mark is a remarkable accomplishment in itself. But what sets her apart in a community that for years has been one of the most isolated in that section of the mountains is the fact that in all her long life she has probably never been farther than twenty miles from the place where she was born, and actually has never seen a hard-surface road. Only once (and that was thirty-five or forty years ago) has she visited her county seat, Brevard, which was then but a small village. In that day the roads into Brevard were little more than trails. Dr. Cannon remembers coming from Brevard over the road she traveled:

"I drove an A-Model Ford, and even that high-axled car had tough going in negotiating mountain roads, particularly when the weather was bad. And even the road from Brevard down to Rosman—now a section of U S Highway 64—was a muddy narrow trail, virtually impassable in rainy weather. In places the mud was knee-deep, and farmers along the road did a flourishing business pulling cars from the mud with teams of horses. It was five dollars a pull-out—I well remember that—and sometimes along that ten-mile stretch you'd have to get pulled out four or five times. That, of course, was back in the 1920s. Since then North Carolina has been building an extensive system of excellent highways, thousands of miles of which have been in the mountain counties. But Aunt Mary, say members of her family, has never even seen one of these roads."

Mrs. McCall's husband died many years ago. He was a farmer and logger in the community, what they call a timber man. Dr. Cannon's father treated him and his wife long before the son can remember, but the old lady clearly recalls the older doctor.

"Your pa holp me many a time," she often tells Gaine Cannon. "If'n you can help me as much as he done, then I'll be all right. Your pa was the finest doctor ever been round these parts. I ain't asayin' you ain't a good one, too, Doctor, but if'n you get to be half as good a doctor or as fine a man as your pa, then you'll be adoin' fine." And many an old man or woman in a cabin deep in some cove will agree with Aunt Mary.

"We had got this booklet out just before I left for Africa,"

Dr. Cannon explains, "and I had told one of our trustees to give out copies through the community. I didn't know that this furor about it was going on until I returned home, when I learned that some of the aggrieved ones had taken a petition through the neighborhood, trying to get the people to sign. The petition offered several proposals, one of which was that I leave Balsam Grove. So I had the meeting called at the schoolhouse; I wanted to answer any questions anyone asked about the booklet, or anything else that I might be able to enlighten them about. I revealed to them that I hadn't written the offending booklet, that it had been written by one of my good friends, but I made it very plain that I was taking responsibility for everything it said. And it was after I had done this that the woman challenged me.

"She didn't appear entirely satisfied with my answer concerning the diets of many of our people. 'Dr. Cannon,' she persisted, 'what percentage of the people in the community, would you say, live like you have described—are illiterate and have inadequate diets, and so on?'

" 'I can't say,' I answered, 'but you can't justify that sort of thing even if the percentage is small. If we have only *one* family like that in our community, we have a problem that we must do something about. We may have ten per cent illiteracy in one community and only one per cent in another. But that doesn't mean that we can be complacent in the one per cent community; we must do something about that *one* per cent. We can't compare this community with another where conditions are worse; we must improve the situation in every community. And another thing,' I went on, 'I want to tell you this right now. It makes no difference what you have been saying about me or will be saying, I'm still your doctor. If you want me in the middle of the night, I'll be here for you to call me. I'm not getting angry; I'll still look after you as long as I'm here; you can depend on that.' "

The next day after the meeting the woman who had criticized him so vehemently took a truck to Brevard and begged from the stores there a load of secondhand furniture. At the schoolhouse meeting the doctor had referred to a family that was living in a shack with virtually no furniture. They were sleeping on the floor, for there was not a bed in the house, and they had only two broken-down chairs. This woman took the furniture to the destitute family. She had experienced a change of heart after coming to the meeting; actually, Dr. Cannon knew, she was a goodhearted soul; she just had not known what the situations were in so many homes in Balsam Grove. Having found out from the doctor about this one, she had proceeded at once to do something about it.

But though a large percentage of the mountain families have very small incomes and many are actually destitute, few ask for help. The people of the highlands possess an inherent pride to which can be traced their fierce independence. They have a strong feeling for family, too, and certain enmities between families have persisted from one generation to another until the reasons for the original ill feelings are no longer known. In the Balsam Grove community are some family feuds comparable almost to the longer persisting and more widely known enmity between the Hatfields and the McCoys; but fortunately, in recent years, Dr. Cannon understands, there have been no killings, although members of the feuding families have occasionally taken pot shots at one another.

"We did have a shooting at Balsam Grove recently that might easily have been a tragedy, though I think it was not a feud shooting," Gaine Cannon recalls. "One of the boys involved, the fellow who got shot, was Vernon McCall, the fellow Peggy Cowart pulled from the river. And on this occasion, like the night he fell into the stream, Vernon was pretty high on mountain corn whiskey.

"He had gone to visit a neighbor boy, a youngster of sixteen or seventeen, and after a while the two had got into an argument that soon became violent. Vernon, strange to report, decided to forego fighting or further discussion and go home. So he had stalked out and closed the door behind him.

"But before Vernon had stepped off the porch, the other boy grabbed a shotgun and blasted a hole through the door as large as a Stayman Winesap apple. It was a bull's-eye shot, too; a bunch of the pellets struck Vernon in the neck and back of the head. If they hadn't spent most of their force in going through the door, I'm sure they'd have blown his head off."

A few minutes after the shooting Vernon appeared at Dr. Cannon's to have the physician cut the shot out.

"I can't do that, Vernon," said Dr. Cannon after he had examined the wounded youth. "I'd just cut your neck all to pieces and then I wouldn't find half of the shots, and you'd be bleeding all over the place. Just forget about those shots; just leave them in there. They aren't going to hurt you, and some of them will work out anyway."

The boy who shot Vernon was described by the doctor as being not "right bright," as they express it in the mountains. He revealed his condition to the doctor, in fact, not long after one of the sheriff's deputies arrived at Balsam Grove; the officer came to Dr. Cannon's to have the physician describe Vernon's injury. The youth, like Vernon, was quite drunk, as well as mentally ill. This was immediately evident when the deputy and the doctor confronted him in his house a little later. "I ain't shot nobody," he declared, "not nary soul, I ain't."

But his mother refused to remain silent. "Son, you did," she contradicted him. "You know you done it. I had the shells hid, but I plumb forgot the one in the gun. You grabbed it up and shot him right through the door."

"Maw, you're alyin'," he stormed. "I didn't shoot nobody. I ain't shot nobody."

"Now, Son, you know you done it," his mother insisted. "And after you shot him, then you jumped on me and hurt me up pretty bad, too." She rolled up her sleeves and showed the officer and the physician marks on her wrist and arm where he had grabbed her and slung her around as she had grabbed for the shotgun.

"Maw, I never done it. You know you're alyin' on me, Maw."

Dr. Cannon was both annoyed and disturbed. "Well, I'll tell you one thing," he declared to the young man, "you're either going to jail or you're going to a mental hospital for treatment. You are not going to stay around here and run loose so you can shoot somebody else, if I have anything to do with it."

The boy turned on him. "Doc, them five pigs what you sold me weren't no good."

"I'd never sold him any pigs, of course," Dr. Cannon said later. "In fact, I'd never sold anybody a pig, or owned one. The boy clearly was mentally ill. His shooting at Vernon was not the first time he had leveled his gun at someone. He and his brother, before the brother was sent to the penitentiary, used to shoot at each other; they'd have a shooting scrape over there every once in a while."

This youth's brother went to the penitentiary for running

a big road-building machine, a bulldozer or an earth mover, over a cliff and dropping it several hundred feet down the mountainside. There had been an earth slide across the road that made driving along it extremely dangerous, and for that reason the road people had parked a heavy machine at each end of the slide with a sign explaining that the road was closed for repairs. When this boy's brother and another young fellow, both drunk, had come along and seen the bulldozer blocking their way, they were enraged; they were too drunk to realize that the machine had been put there for their protection.

So these boys had cross-wired one of the machines (they had tried to cross-wire the other, but had failed), started the motor, put the machine in gear, and run it over the cliff. It was badly damaged, of course; it cost two or three thousand dollars to get it back up to the highway and repaired. Since the offense had occurred in Pisgah National Forest, the FBI came out and investigated, and took fingerprints. But they had not been able to apprehend the boys immediately; this one's brother got a pup tent and fled back into the mountains.

"Friends would take him food," Gaine Cannon reveals, "and he had his girl friend with him part of the time he was hiding out. But one day some FBI men walked up on him, and his camping out was ended. The court sent him to a mental hospital. He's still there. But when he gets out, the brothers likely will start potshoting at each other again."

Although life in the mountains, rigorous as it still is, has mellowed somewhat in recent years as good roads and schools and the other accouterments of advancing civilization have pushed far up into the hills, sometimes Gaine Cannon encounters characters that remind him of folk he met when once he visited in the home of a fellow student at Berea College.

This boy lived near Pound, Virginia, in the Blue Ridge Mountains. Pound has been recently in the news as the home town of Gary Powers, the American pilot who was forced down while flying an intelligence mission over the Soviet Union and was sentenced to ten years in prison, from which a year or so later he was released and returned to the United States.

"My classmate had been urging me to visit him," Gaine Cannon relates. "So one year between the ending of summer school and the beginning of the fall term I decided to go up to Pound. I rode the train as far as I could, and then hired a taxi to take me to the end of the road leading to my friend's home; there was no road into the place.

" 'It's none of my business, mister,' said the taxi driver when I got out, 'but where are you agoin'?'

" 'I'm going to visit Bill Wright,' I told him. 'They said I'd have to walk from here across over that mountain.'

" 'I know him,' the driver said. 'He's a son of old man John Wright. Mister'—his expression and tone were serious—'you ain't agoin' up there to see *him*, are you?'

" 'Yes,' I told him.

"He shook his head solemnly. 'Mister, I don't want to worry you none,' he confided, 'but if you go up there to old man John Wright's, you won't be acomin' back alive.' His eyes narrowed and his forehead furrowed. 'Did you know that old man John Wright, he's done killed twenty-six men a'ready?' He rubbed his balding pate, from which he had removed his wool hat. 'And, mister, he ain't never made no time for it.'

"Well, for a while I thought that there was a good chance that the fellow's ominous prediction would be borne out. As I trudged up that twisting path across Burnt Mountain and along Killing Trail—those actually were the names—I was stopped several times by people who asked me brusquely, as they held me at gunpoint, what my business was in those parts. I hasten to add that I didn't hesitate in telling them. I'm sure they thought that I just might be a 'revenuer.' I evidently convinced them that I wasn't; if I hadn't, doubtless the taxi driver's prediction would have come true on the spot."

Finally Gaine Cannon reached the Wright place unscathed and met old Mr. Wright and other members of the family. His friend Bill Wright had told him that John Fox, Jr., in writing his best-selling novel, *The Trail of the Lonesome Pine*, had used his father as the prototype of his principal character, Devil Judd, father of June, the heroine. It was hard for young Cannon, however, to see in old Mr. Wright the rough and ruthless Devil Judd. But Mr. Wright, then past eighty, had indeed killed twenty-six or more men, though most of them had been killed after the Civil War period in line of duty while he was serving as deputy sheriff. But to Gaine Cannon he was both hospitable and courteous. Nevertheless, the old man was a rugged character; he was living with one woman on one side of the creek and another on the other side, and the two women were but a stone's throw apart. Young Cannon thought that to be able to do that was in itself quite an accomplishment. He was told that Mr. Wright had thirty-two children, but he did not inquire as to how they were distributed between the two women and/or others, or what the distribution was with respect to birth in or out of wedlock. He did, however, ask his friend Bill where the thirty-two offspring of his father were at that time.

"Oh, two or three are in insane asylums," Bill replied nonchalantly, "and two or three are in the penitentiary, and two or three are making moonshine, and two or three are dead"—he paused, his brow wrinkled in concentration—"and I just be darned if I know where the rest of 'em are."

It has been many years since Gaine Cannon visited his college friend in Virginia, and he has not seen the John Fox, Jr., novel in all that time, but he does remember that the action of the novel and the description of the characters follow very much the life story of the family he was visiting.

"I recall that we trudged up the trail of the lonesome pine to the pine itself. The pine had been cut down, but the stump was there. And we saw Killing Rock, where seven persons were killed, and other places referred to in the novel, and I was told how Fox in his narrative had followed with little variation the course of actual happenings in that section of the Virginia mountains.

"The day we went up the trail in search of the lonesome pine, I also recall, 'where you carved your sweetheart's name and I carved mine,' we heard somebody singing; it was a man's voice, and it was growing louder.

"Bill listened a moment. 'I know who it is,' he said. 'He's a moonshiner; we'll go on down there and I'll show you. In a few minutes he'll be coming along on a little mule, with a five-gallon keg swinging in a sack on each side, and he'll offer us a drink. But actually he'll be taking that whiskey down to the highway, where somebody will meet him and take it to sell it.'

"We went on down the trail, and sure enough, he came along, riding a mule, with a keg in a sack on each side. He stopped, said hello to Bill, and nodded to me. 'Well, boys,' he said, and I saw at once that he himself was feeling no pain, 'how about a drink?' He was turning around to untie the sack, but Bill thanked him and told him we wouldn't have one. He knew that the fellow had arranged to sell the whiskey, so he wouldn't be offended at our refusal. He wasn't, and in another minute he was off again on his mule, and down the trail a little way he was once more singing at the top of his voice."

Now Pound, Virginia, is a much larger place. Good roads and good schools and advancing times have changed conditions. And so it is at Balsam Grove. "Time changes things," Gaine Cannon agrees. "Even people. Sometimes I wonder if it's always for the best. Certainly it has taken away and failed to replace many delightfully unique characters. People like old man Wright. People like Cannon McCall and Aunt Corrie, and Aunt Carnettie. And our mountains, for me, at any rate, won't be at their best without them."

CHAPTER

II

BUT passing time and changing conditions have done little to alter the personalities of these charming older folk in the mountains, Gaine Cannon happily has discovered. And one of the qualities he most admires in them and feels has had much to do with their attaining to remarkable old age is what he calls their spirit of reverence for life.

There is the old man, for instance, who lives away over in Jackson County, some thirty-five miles from Balsam Grove. Dr. Cannon tells about him:

"I had a call to go to see this old gentleman, who was then eighty-two. He was having convulsions every few minutes and his family expected him to die momentarily. In fact, they told me frankly they had had three doctors come out from the county seat to see him; the last one had said, 'There's no use in my coming again because it's only a matter of hours, or at the most a day or two, before he dies.'

"I thought so too when I arrived there and examined the old man, but I didn't tell the family that because I never tell anyone or his family that he's going to die. I've had so many patients tell me 'Old Dr. So-and-So told me twenty years ago that I had two months to live, and he's been dead a long time now and I'm still going strong' that it has made me wary of forecasting the time of a patient's death.

"When I got to him, the patient was having one attack after another and it looked like each one might be the last. I stayed with him two or three hours, and finally he began to get better, temporarily, I thought to myself. I told his wife quite frankly that he was critically ill and anything could happen, though I did not tell her that I thought he was going to die, and soon. And when I left I felt certain that I'd never see him again alive.

"But the next Monday—I was making calls into Jackson County every Monday—when I went back to his house I found him sitting up in bed, much better. 'Doc,' he said to me, 'one of these days pretty soon I want you to come over and go asquirrel huntin' with me.' I agreed to go, but I had no idea I ever would, of course.

"Well, I kept going to see this old gentleman, and some Mondays when Dr. Edens went on those Jackson County calls he'd go by to call on him. Some days he would have six or eight convulsions, they called them; he'd shake, and stop breathing, and turn blue and black in the face. I'd give him an injection and some medicine; the injection would cause relaxation of the blood vessels that permitted more blood to get to the heart. The patient also had a severe cough and was continuously giving up phlegm and blood from the chest. We were able, fortunately, to get a nurse in the neighborhood to give him penicillin and streptomycin every day for five days. This treatment cleared his chest condition; he stopped coughing and spitting up blood, and began to get noticeably better. The next time I was up there he was sitting on the porch.

"But the old gentleman continued to have convulsions every few days, and we greatly feared he would die. We got the nurse to attend him again and give him injections for his heart and to improve his circulation. For three or four weeks I didn't see him, though I received reports on him. In that time he was much better; his wife told me that he was walking about the house, eating his meals at the table. Then one day he walked out into the yard and climbed up and down the steps, which were high, several times. I received an emergency call to see him. He had overexerted himself, of course, and this had called on his heart for more blood, and he had started having attacks again. When I went into his room he was lying in bed, but he was in good spirits and knew what he was saying and doing. "I'm not ready to go asquirrel huntin' today, Doc," he announced, "but I think I'm gettin' better, and maybe we can go the next time you come over."

"I treated him and he responded quickly. I haven't seen him since, but I continue to hear from him. Recently he sent me word again that he was ready to go on that squirrel hunt. He may die any day, and he may live several years. I think my medicine has helped him, of course, but I feel that a larger contribution toward keeping him alive has been his spirit. Much depends, I am convinced, on a patient's wanting to live, being determined to live, and knowing that others want him to live. I believe, too, that such a feeling is communicated, and that there are a lot of people who die before their time because no one encourages them to live. As Dr. Schweitzer says, you see a man who is about to lose his will to live, and he may do it unless someone comes along and gives assistance to this faltering will. I think that doctors and medicine and good nursing care are very important, but there must be something else if the patient is to be cured. He must have the will to live, and he must know that someone else shares with him that reverence for his life.

"All through life there's a will to live, especially in humans, but the strength of this will varies in individuals. I believe that no sane person wills to die, that all persons who commit suicide are to some degree mentally ill. But sometimes one's will to live diminishes, sometimes it falters, and it is then most important that someone else do something to strengthen and revive this impoverished will.

"I have noticed this will to live, too, in many patients who had incurable diseases; often it carries them on for months after they were expected to die. A good example of this was the late Speaker Sam Rayburn. He had a cancer and knew that he was going to die. But he carried on to the last; he went out and made speeches after he knew that he had this incurable disease. By his example he was helping other people to express their wills to live. He had spent a long life working for people, helping them express their wills to live, and his last days were simply a continuation of that effort.

"Many people, I believe, do indeed die before their time; they lie down and die, often after periods of considerable suffering, when they might have lived longer and more happily and died with their boots on, as the expression goes, if they had really been determined to live longer. I am confident that a patient's mental condition has much to do with his physical well-being. I have known of many persons, some of them my patients, who lived ten or fifteen years after they had been given up to die within a month or two. I recall the story told by the late Dr. Mary Martin Sloop, herself a mountain physician who achieved national fame for her work as a doctor and educator at Crossnore, in the North Carolina Blue Ridge, and was the American Mother of the Year in 1951.

"In 1911, Dr. Sloop said, she and her husband, also a physician, sent a mountain woman to a hospital several counties away to have her ailment diagnosed. The report came back that she had an abdominal cancer and would die likely within two months. But the woman had no notion of dying. In fact, she did not die until 1957, I believe, at the age of about ninety. The diagnosis had been correct; an exploratory operation revealed a cancer far advanced. What happened? A miracle, some would say, or perhaps it was her will to live."

Dr. Cannon tells another story, this one about a woman who was sent from South Carolina to the Mayo Clinic. Her doctor thought she had a malignancy, but did not tell her. But when this cancer was discovered by the doctors at Mayo, they told her, and they said further that she would live about two months. She telephoned her South Carolina physician and weepingly related what the doctors there had told her.

"Listen, Mary," her doctor said when he had calmed her enough for her to hear what he was saying, "if you don't shut up that crying and come on home, you won't live two months. You must come home now and make the best of the time you have left, and maybe you'll have a lot more than you think you will now."

The woman recovered her courage, came home, and set out to make the most of the time left her. Ten years after the delivery of the two-month death sentence she was still living, busily and happily teaching school. That was the last Dr. Cannon heard of her.

"For all I know," he says, "she may be living now. She got her courage back, her will to live, she knew that others were anxious for her to live, and she lived. Sometimes it is just that simple."

In further substantiation of his contention that a person's will to live works powerfully toward keeping him alive, Dr. Cannon relates the story of a wealthy man who, years ago, had a very advanced stomach ulcer:

"Surgery for such cases had not been perfected and operations were not often attempted, and then only in extreme cases. This man had a bleeding ulcer. His doctors, a general practitioner, a diagnostician, and a stomach specialist, had been seeing him every day, and they had agreed that nothing further could be done for him. The ulcer was inoperable, they said, and they notified him that he had only a few months to live.

"He received the verdict calmly, thought about it without panicking, and when the next day they came to see him he greeted them cheerfully. 'Gentlemen,' he said, 'you have told me that I have six months to live. During that time, you have also told me, you would have to put a tube into my stomach and wash it out every day. Well, gentlemen, let me tell you that that won't be necessary. I have been working hard for a long time, and most of that time I've been under a nervous tension as I drove myself in my business. But I have managed to make and save some money. All the time I have been working hard, too, I have been looking forward to the time when I could retire and do some traveling. All my life, for example, I have wanted to visit the Orient, go to China and Japan and other countries in the East. And now that the time when I can retire has arrived, you tell me that I have but these few months to live.

" 'Well, gentlemen, you can forget about washing out my stomach every day. I'm going on that trip. Yesterday after you gave me your verdict I telephoned and engaged passage.' He told them the name of the ship.

" 'But you can't do that!' one of the doctors declared. 'You'll die on board ship, and they'll have to bury you at sea.'

"The man held up his hand firmly. 'No, Doctor," he said, 'I'm going. And I've already made arrangements with the skipper of the ship that if I die he'll have my body placed in cold storage until the ship returns home and it can be buried here. I'll take the stomach pump along and I'll pump out my stomach myself.'

"When the man went aboard ship, he promptly threw the stomach pump away. He stopped worrying, and his tenseness soon vanished. He traveled throughout the Orient, had an exciting and most pleasant trip, and came home in a stateroom and not the ship's cooler. Years later, the last I heard of him, he was back in business and enjoying excellent health.

"This man had just decided that during the months he had to live he would live. He lost his fear, he relaxed, he began to enjoy himself, and his ulcer healed. It was simply a case of mind prevailing over matter. Now, I don't believe in any hocus-pocus or miraculous cures, but I do believe that if a man quits, gives up, throws in the towel, pretty soon he's dead. On the other hand, he can fight on, with all the odds against him, apparently, he can lose all and start over from the beginning; his head may be bloody, as the poem says, but unbowed, and he can get well. I believe that there are untold, unknown, almost unimagined possibilities locked up in the breast of every human being. But he must call upon them if he is to use them. Dr. Schweitzer says that if you can get a man to think you have won half the battle. If he thinks inwardly, he unlocks all kinds of possibilities. Most of the things, good or bad, that have happened to the world have happened because of individuals who have meditated. There is Jesus of Nazareth. Think what His meditating, His inward thinking has done for the world. Or on the dark side it may be a Hitler or a Mussolini or an Alexander the Great, who killed millions of people. But in each case a person's inward thinking did it.

"The world is filled with individuals," Dr. Cannon says, "who have accomplished what the world describes as miracles. 'As a [man] thinketh in his heart, so is he.' It is indeed the individual himself who does something. Nowhere can you find a group that is doing anything remarkable unless it is led by an individual who has thought out a course of action. This is a world of individuals, and untold possibilities lie within an individual. I firmly believe that if the individual stops and thinks seriously 'What can I do?' and then declares 'I'll do this' or 'I'll do that' and meditates upon it and works at it with determination, he will in all probability do it. I have seen it happen many times."

The Balsam Grove physician delights in revealing case histories of such patients whom he has treated during his years of service in the mountains.

"I've had a number of patients who were thought to be on their last legs," he says. "They had been told that they were going to die momentarily, and their families were prepared for their going. I remember particularly an old lady past ninety who had had at least three doctors tell her family that there was nothing they could do for her, that she might die any minute.

"They asked me to see her, though she does not live in the section I cover regularly. So I went to see her, and I agreed with the doctors who had been treating her. I didn't see how she could live much longer. She was unconscious; for some time she hadn't taken a drop of nourishment. She weighed only about eighty pounds; she was extremely dehydrated; you could pick her skin up and pull it three or four inches from

" 'And whoever compels you to go a mile with him, go with him two miles.' That is the gist of Dr. Schweitzer's philosophy and it's mine."

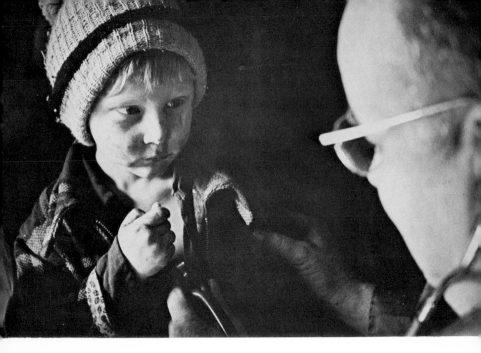

"My office hours are day and night throughout the week."

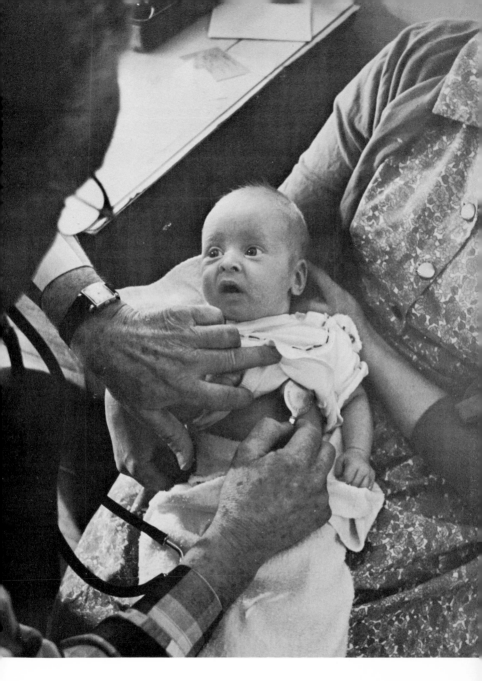

"They bundle up the sick babies and bring them over to Balsam Grove."

"There are very few places that 'Old Faithful' can't get to."

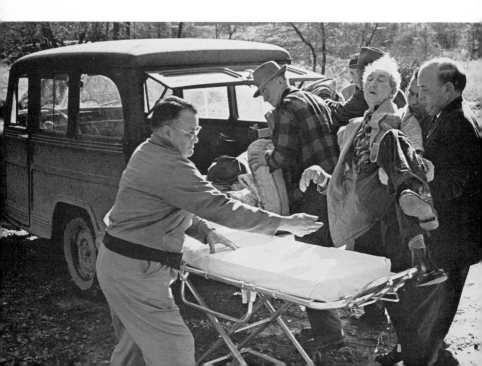

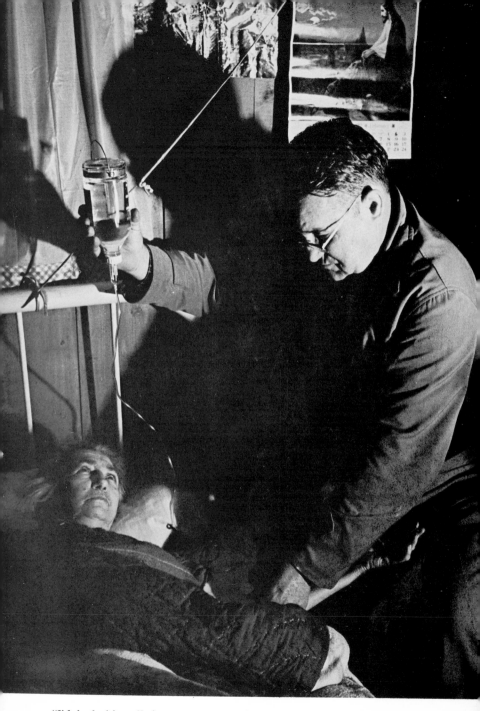

"I'd had this call from away over in Jackson County. An elderly woman was desperately ill. Could I possibly come? I told them I'd try."

"Passing time and changing conditions have done little to alter the personalities of these charming older folk in the mountains."

"I love these people.
They're my folk."

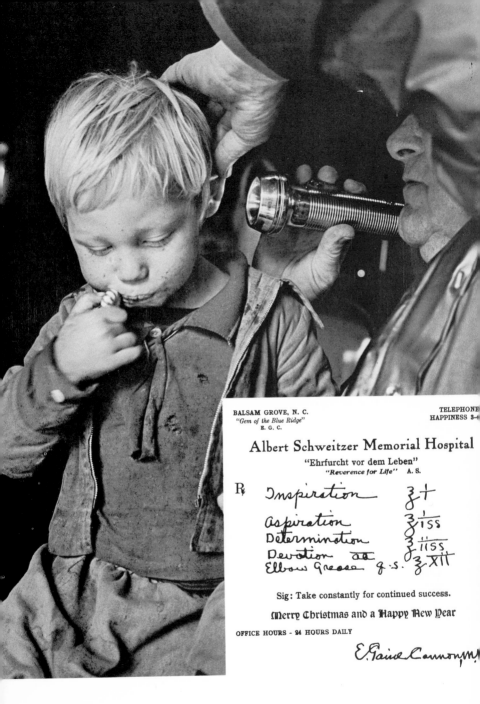

BALSAM GROVE, N. C.
"*Gem of the Blue Ridge*"
B. G. C.

TELEPHONE
HAPPINESS 3-

Albert Schweitzer Memorial Hospital

"*Ehrfurcht vor dem Leben*"
"*Reverence for Life*" A. S.

R℞ Inspiration ... ʒ+
Aspiration ... ʒ¹⁄₁₅₅
Determination ... ʒ¹⁄₁₅₅
Devotion āā ... ʒ·s· ʒXII
Elbow Grease q.s.

Sig: Take constantly for continued success.

Merry Christmas and a Happy New Year

OFFICE HOURS - 24 HOURS DAILY

E. Gaine Cannon M.

"I originally came up to Balsam Grove to rest."

her arms. I didn't see how I could do anything for her, but I thought I would try, at least, out of my reverence for life."

So Dr. Cannon had his nurse go to the old woman's home and give her a quart of glucose loaded with vitamins.

"Put into the veins, it went right into the blood; it didn't have to be digested. It gave a ready nutriment and fluids that she badly needed. Soon after she'd had that quart of glucose she began taking a little water; before that she had strangled when we put a few drops into her mouth. A little later she was able to take a small amount of ice cream with chocolate syrup on it, and then other vitamins in liquid form by mouth. Next she was able to eat a soft egg, and other things, like Jell-O. Now, two months later, she's still living, and much improved. She knows members of the family, talks with them, quarrels with them sometimes when they don't please her, laughs and even tells a joke now and then. And truly, if anyone ever had a foot in the grave, it was this old lady.

"Now, in her case I do not think that at first it was her will to live that saved her life. She was past that. She was unconscious, and I believe, had no idea of existence or anything else; she was just vegetating. What she needed was fluid and nourishment, which the glucose and vitamins provided, and that tipped the scales. But pretty soon she came to the point where she did know something, and she wanted to live, was determined to live, and in my opinion, it was that will to live that brought about her steady improvement."

The old lady began to ask for her children, to inquire where each was, Dr. Cannon noticed in his visits to her; she began to experience pain, to take on life again. "And although she was in bed, and had been in bed almost four months when she began to show steady improvement, she had been so well taken care of that she had developed no bed sores, which old people long in bed customarily develop. Now she is much better, has gained a little weight, her skin isn't so loose, she's no longer dehydrated, and they can set her up on the side of the bed. She'll never jump rope again, and she'll never square dance, or do anything like that, and though they may have to spoon-feed her the rest of her life, they will have her for a while longer, and they are happy for it. I believe that not only my treatment helped bring her around, but that also little things I did, like encouraging her family not to give her up, showing them how to do small chores to help her, giving her a few drops of this, a few drops of that every ten or fifteen minutes, talking cheerfully to her and in her hearing. I think these little things helped nourish her will to live and keep her alive two months after she had been given up to die.

"For a while I saw her every two or three days, even though she lived in a community considerably distant from Balsam Grove; now they call me when she needs me, and I keep in touch with her even when I don't go to see her. I do all I can to bolster her will to live; in turn, her example has been an inspiration to me."

Gaine Cannon's reverence for life, his abhorrence of the taking of life, particularly human life, adds to the natural aversion of a physician to performing an abortion on an expectant mother.

"People ask me what is my feeling about it in the cases of the pregnant women who have been treated with the drug Thalidomide. The cases of the woman in Belgium and the American young woman in Arizona who went abroad for an abortion have naturally caused much talk. It's a difficult question. I can understand why a woman who feels sure that she is going to have a horribly deformed baby would seek an abortion, and I sympathize with her. And when the mother thinks it will be a mental cripple, a living human vegetable, malformed and without a mind, I know there's nothing more terrible. I see it as a question of reverence for life, and my first thought is for the mother when it's a question of the mother or the unborn child. The unborn child knows nothing about life and has no thoughts, I'm confident, but certainly the mother does, and to know that she must live long years with a horribly deformed baby, a child without arms, for instance, or even worse, without a functioning mind, must be hell on earth. And yet to take a life, any sort of life, any sort of human life, to me is not man's prerogative. That is God's prerogative.

"And what of the baby without arms, the malformed child? What of the baby himself?

"I know a man today who was born without arms. A hopeless cripple, they doubtless said of him when he was born, a malformed creature who would be better off dead. Yet today this man can play a guitar with his feet; many times he has played on radio and television. He drives his car with his feet —he has a special state license and he passed a driving test to get it. He does about everything that a man with hands does, and he does it with gusto and enjoyment. I have eaten with him at the table. He takes off his shoes, picks up his fork between the toes of one foot and his knife between the toes of the other foot, cuts his steak or whatever may require cutting, and eats. He loves his life and lives it fully. It would have been a tragedy to deprive that baby of his right to life simply because he was malformed."

On the other hand, Dr. Cannon speaks of another man— man in years—who has the mind of a year-old baby.

"Twenty-four hours a day, every day of every week since he was born," Gaine Cannon says, "someone, usually his mother or one of his sisters, holds that man-baby in her arms, on her lap. If she indicates that she is about to put him down, he whimpers and cries. He is just like a suckling babe. There are several excellent brothers and sisters in this family, including grown daughters with husbands of substantial means. Yet such is the reverence for life within the family group, particularly among the mother and sisters, that this poor imbecilic child-man has lavished upon him almost all the family's care and attention.

"It is a remarkable thing to see, but often in the mountains I come upon a child who, though mentally he may have the comprehension of an infant, is large and strong physically; in fact, some of them, though mentally having the age of three or four, may be grown men or women weighing sometimes two hundred fifty to three hundred pounds. Most of these unfortunates are the results of accidents at birth, or more probably, of intermarriage of near relatives. In isolated communities we have a lot of intermarriage of first cousins. Sometimes when the families are strong, it produces exceptional offspring, but more often it simply doubles the weaknesses and produces inferior children. Such marriages disregard the rules of heredity and the good life; they manifest, as I see it, a contempt for the proper life, a lack of reverence, if you will, for life."

So Gaine Cannon reasons that evils of every sort are spawned through this lack of reverence for life, as he defines it, this absence of *"Ehrfurcht vor dem Leben."*

"And," he says, "it is a great pity. If we had more reverence for life among races and among nations, we could have a vastly different world. That's the thing that will end the cold war and prevent another hot war, not only reverence for your own life and your family's or your countrymen's, but for all the people in all the world, for all the life in all the world. It's a mysterious and a marvelous thing to me that everything that lives wants to live. All life runs from danger; it flees from death; it matters not whether it's the tiniest insect or an animal or man. And man, the highest of the creatures, is the only one that wilfully destroys its life. And as I have said, no sane person, in my opinion, ever kills himself. He may be a brilliant man, but I firmly believe he must be deranged before he commits suicide. A man can think, he has a conscience, he can be happy or unhappy. I think an animal is neither happy nor unhappy, however; I believe he is simply physically satisfied and comfortable or dissatisfied—hungry, for instance—or uncomfortable. But within him, as within man, is this desire to live. And all other conscious life, I feel with Dr. Schweitzer, should respect and encourage this reverence for life."

CHAPTER

12

ONE of the pleasant results of Dr. Cannon's visit to the old Jackson County native critically ill of a heart disorder and his subsequent setting aside Mondays for calls into that county was his discovery of a man whom he would soon add to his list of favorite mountain characters.

"He was a tall, lanky fellow with a big grin that revealed a few tobacco-stained, snaggly teeth," the doctor describes him, "and he lived over near Tuckaseigee. His house soon became an assembly point for patients from that section who gathered there for my Monday visits. People would come from as far away as Webster and Sylva, the county seat, and Cullowhee, where they have a large state teachers college. Sometimes a patient would be unable to get out of the car in which a relative or neighbor had brought him, and I'd give him emergency treatment in the vehicle, which frequently was a pickup truck. Often there'd be a half dozen or more patients collected at this man's house when I arrived, and it was a great convenience for both them and me, because it enabled me to see more people than if I had been forced to go to each one's home. Even then I often made from fifteen to twenty home calls on a Monday, and those traveling over sometimes almost impassable mountain roads.

"This man's function, on the days I was seeing patients congregated at his house, a self-appointed chore, I might point out, was to entertain these folk while they waited their turn with the doctor. Whenever I could, I listened in on his storytelling. He was amazingly good at it, a sort of mountaineer Will Rogers. He himself was usually the subject of his unsophisticated but devastating satire. And as Will Rogers said he did, this Jackson County wit apparently liked everybody he ever saw."

For years this man's father, though not a trained physician, had been the only doctor the community boasted. He had treated enough cattle and people, however, to be given the title of "Doc," and he had actually been given a limited license by the state to practice medicine. That was in the days when doctors trained in medical schools were not available in many isolated communities, and therefore licenses of this kind were issued to midwives or other skilled in delivering babies and treating people with herb teas and other such home remedies. The elder man's treatments had never been known to kill anyone or otherwise do him damage; in fact, he was beloved in his community as a man who had done much good and helped cure the ills and relieve the suffering of many of his folk.

"When this 'doc' died," Gaine Cannon says, "the people of the community transferred the title to his son, who from time to time had helped his father in his simple ministering to their ailments. So he treated them for their colds and their rheumatism and their injuries, if they were not serious, and they had much faith in him, as they had had in his father.

"But one day a man came to him while he was at work on his regular job at one of the mines.

[151]

" 'Listen, Doc,' the fellow said, 'my wife is agoin' to have a baby pretty soon, and I wonder if you'll look after her.'

" 'Yeh,' he said, 'I'll be glad to. Just let me know when you'll be aneedin' me.'

" 'But right then I knew I wasn't agoin' to do it,' this amateur doctor told us one day when I was over at his house. 'I knew I couldn't deliver no baby. I didn't know nothin' about doin' a job like that. And the more I thought about it, the scareder I got. So the next mornin' I went to the foreman. I told him I wanted my time, that I was aleavin'.' "

The foreman, Gaine Cannon continues, was surprised.

" 'How come you're aleavin'?' he inquired. 'Ain't we been atreatin' you right?'

" 'Sure, you been atreatin' me fine,' the quitting employee assured him. 'I ain't aleavin' on account o' how you been atreatin' me.'

" 'Well, what's the matter?' the foreman persisted.

" 'A man asked me to deliver his wife; she's agoin' to have a baby in a few days. And I can't do it, and I ain't agoin' to try to. But I don't want him to know it. I done got my suitcase packed; I'm apullin' out.' "

And that's what he did. He stayed away until after the baby was born.

"He's full of stories," Gaine Cannon says. "He's had almost every kind of experience, has worked in many parts of the country. He built the first bridge over the river in his section. He remembers, he says, when there were forty bridges over that stream, and now there are only two. He recalls the big flood—it must have been in 1916—that did such destruction. He can tell in detail of the frightful days when the roaring waters washed away everything in their path. And nowhere have I heard or read a more dramatic account of it than his."

But this Jackson County citizen possesses another ability that excites Gaine Cannon's interest.

"He's an inventor, too, and his inventions cover a wide, and strange, range. One day when I was over at his place he said to me, 'Doc, I want to tell you 'bout this invention I've got. The patent's apendin', and the only reason I ain't already put it on the market is because I haven't found anybody who'll make me a little motor to run it with. But I'll get one 'fore long. What it is, Doc, is a churn, and it's a danged good 'ne. It'll churn butter in three minutes by the clock, and by golly, Doc, that's achurnin'. Course you can run it by hand like it is, but it'd be a lot better to have a motor on it and some day 'fore too long I'm agoin' to find me somebody to make me a little motor like what I want, and then there's no tellin' how many of them churns I'll be asellin'!"

He got the churn out and showed it to Dr. Cannon; the doctor was impressed. "I believe when he gets that motor rigged up to it," he says, "that churn will bring butter in two minutes instead of three! It's a simple contraption with a dasher that goes down in it and has three different motions. Instead of going only up and down, the dasher goes around, up and down, and out and back sideways. It was a marvel to me. I hope he gets the motor; I'd like to see it hooked up to that churn."

Even more intriguing to Dr. Cannon was another device the man showed him. But first he excused the women from the room. "Doc, it's a slick little thing made out of wood," he explained when they had gone, "and it's no trouble to sterilize it. What it's for is to help relieve a woman who has got a womb that's fell. You put it in position and you turn a little screw and it opens up and just pushes and lifts that womb back in place. In just a jiffy she's rid of all the symptoms of a fallen womb, Doc, and all that pullin'-down, pressin'-on-the-bladder feelin', because her womb's been pushed back where it b'longs. Yes, sir, Doc, when I get that motor made for the churn and get it and this here thing on the market, I'll be asellin' a right smart of them both. I got a good doctor friend that told me—he died last year, but he told me 'fore he died—that if I had this little thing on the market he'd buy three hundred of 'em right off. He must a had a danged lot o' women patients, but that's what he told me."

Dr. Cannon himself believes that his Jackson County friend's inventions, particularly the one for adjusting a fallen womb, has possibilities of success. "Some folk say that if the thing were any good it would have been developed by doctors themselves long before now," he points out, "but I have an idea they said the same thing about other developments in the mechanics of surgery and medicine. I'm thinking, for instance, of the Sims duckbill speculum. Dr. James Marion Sims, born down in Lancaster County, South Carolina, in 1813, invented this instrument, which enabled the surgeon to look into the womb and thereby made possible a tremendous advance in surgery on women patients. After he did it, surgeons wondered why it hadn't been done before. The same thing was true of Dr. Crawford Long of Georgia, who first used ether to anesthetize patients about to undergo surgery. People wondered why somebody hadn't thought of it before Long began to experiment with it. So it may be that this fellow over in Jackson County may have something, or the rough principle of something, that when perfected may prove to be important."

Dr. Cannon reveals how he happened to be treating this mountaineer inventor:

"He had been hurt or suffered an ailment, I forget now

what it was, but at any rate, he had been treated by several doctors, one of whom had put him on narcotics, and unfortunately, he had let drugs get too strong a hold on him. That's when I began treating him, and I've been steadily cutting him down until now he's almost off the habit. I was joking with him one day and I said, 'You know, you're getting along pretty well; I've been cutting down on you and it hasn't been bothering you too much, has it?'

" 'And I've been aknowin' you were acuttin' down on me, too, Doc,' he said, grinning. 'That there nurse wasn't foolin' me none. I been awatchin' her. When she steps out o' the room, I look in that little vial she gets the stuff from for her needle, and I see how much she's left in it, and she's been aleavin' a good deal in that vial, too.' Then he was serious. 'But that's all right, Doc. That's good. I'm gettin' off it, and I'm glad. I'd rather she'd leave the stuff in that vial than put it in my arm. I want to get plumb off the stuff, and I'm agoin' to do it, too.'

"And I am confident he will completely overcome the habit of depending upon this codeine product that for a long time has been a sort of crutch for him," the doctor says. "He is really a fine person as well as a charming and unique individual. And he possesses the will power."

Dr. Cannon has another reason for enjoying his visits to his inventor friend's home, he confesses.

"Whenever I happen to be there at mealtime I have to eat with them. And that's not good for a fellow who is trying to take off pounds. One day they'll have goat meat, and another day it'll be a bear dinner, and the next time they may have vension."

The doctor likes bear meat, but he tries to avoid the fatty portions. "Bear meat, when it's cooked right, is delicious, but it is strong, and usually the mountain folk cook it with considerable fat left on. It should be cooked a long time, and when it is, it is quite tender. Up here in the hills the meat is cooked several ways. First it is parboiled, and then fried or cut up into chunks and cooked in a stew. Bear meat tastes very much like beef, though it has a little more of a wild, earthy flavor. I like it, and when I get a chance to sit down to a bear dinner I generally eat too much. I like venison, too, which also tastes somewhat like beef."

Dr. Cannon is continually fighting to lose weight; sometimes he loses a few pounds, but more often, he confesses, he gains them. "I'm entirely too big around the middle," he readily admits. "But it's a hard, always uphill battle for me to lose weight. If you don't eat with your patients when you're in their homes at mealtimes, they'll be offended. And even between meals you must have a cup of coffee and a piece of cake or a slice of pie, or whatever they happen to have. And naturally"—he grins as he says it—"I never want to offend my friends. But when a mountain family sets you down to the table and a country-style meal, it's generally mighty good eating. City folk, I'm sure, have never eaten beans and cabbage, particularly if they're served in restaurants, like they cook them in the mountains. They put just the right amount of pork in them for seasoning, and in the string beans they cook some shelled beans—'shelly beans,' the folk up here call them—and corn bread and maybe bear meat or venison, and sauerkraut and homemade pickles and raspberry preserves and big, thick hot biscuits and honey and home-churned butter! All that good food makes it mighty hard for me to keep to my dieting routine."

Meals in the homes of most of his patients, those who eat well even though their money earnings may be small, recall for him his childhood days in that same section of the mountains, he says.

"I can remember vividly how my grandmother used to make a pone of corn bread three or four inches thick, put it in a three-legged skillet on the edge of the hearth next to the fire, rake a great pile of glowing coals under the skillet and a layer of coals on the top of the covered skillet, and let it cook there while we warmed by the roaring fire. And sometimes she put cracklings in the bread mixture, and you'd have shortening bread, or what we called crackling bread. Cracklings, I might explain, are the dried-down remains from rendering lard. They are crisp and crunchy, and to me they add immeasurably to the goodness of corn bread made the old-fashioned way. You can sometimes buy cracklings in the stores, put up in packages like dried beans, but they aren't as good as those lifted right out of the iron pot after the lard has been rendered.

"And a big hunk of that crackling corn bread and a tall glass of sweet milk! Man, that is eating. And if you truly want a feast, then add to that warm corn bread and cold sweet milk a plate of good old-fashioned homemade country sorghum so thick you can almost cut 'em with your knife. And I say 'cut them' rather than 'cut it' advisedly. Whoever heard of anybody in our mountains referring to molasses as anything but 'them molasses'? The good old days are slipping away fast, even in Balsam Grove, but I can still take you to many a mountain home where you get that old-time cooking, and as some of our folk say it even yet, those good old-time 'vittles.' "

CHAPTER

13

ONE of the hospitable homes in which sometimes Gaine Cannon eats a meal is the cabin of a very poor family that has suffered much misfortune.

"This is particularly true of the mother," he says. "She is crippled with arthritis; she has been coming to see me and I have been making calls to her home for a long time, and I have tried every way I could to help her. As a child she must have had polio that crippled her, and to make that worse, some years ago she fell and broke one knee all to pieces. Much of the time she has had to hobble about on crutches.

"She has had many other troubles, too," Dr. Cannon continues, "some of them not because of poor health. The family has always been in bad shape financially, and now her children, though grown, give her little help. Her husband has been of little help too; he's a sickly fellow who frequently has 'blind spells' during which he has to be led around. He might be described as an 'inadequate personality,' to put it charitably, a man whose problems so far overreach his capabilities that he succumbs to them; he has fainting spells and falls out. So instead of being a help to his wife he is an added responsibility.

"The other day this woman was seated in my waiting room; her crutches were leaning against her chair. Across from her sat one of my friends from the Piedmont section of the state. The two began to chat, and presently she was telling him of her ailments, including her troublesome 'artheritis' and of my still unsuccessful efforts to cure her.

" 'Then why don't you go see a *good* doctor and let him treat you?' my friend asked, his expression serious.

" 'Well now,' she answered, her eyes flashing, 'I'm acomin' to a *good* doctor now. They ain't no better doctor nowhere than him. Doc Cannon he's holp me more'n any other doctor would a done, I'm a notion.' "

Gaine Cannon has been treating her for years. He has no idea how much she owes him. "Sometimes I put it down in the book, sometimes I don't," he says. "She pays me when she can, but she can't often get any money with which to pay. If anybody needs and deserves welfare help, she does. Some years ago the welfare department gave her a little girl to raise, and this child has been an added responsibility; she has needed medical attention, including an operation on her eye. Yet, the old lady tells me, the welfare people don't give her a cent.

"One day some weeks ago she paid me five dollars on her bill. Last week she was back, and when I had finished with her she said to Helen, 'I wish you'd run up my bill.' Helen did, and on the big book it ran to more than two hundred dollars. 'Don't tell me any more,' she said. 'It'll dishearten me.' Helen said she wouldn't.

"But I'll go out to her house on a call and she'll say, 'Now, Doc, I just made some fresh kraut, and it's good, too.' And she'll call out to the little girl, 'Fay, you run out to the garden and get Doc Cannon some 'matoes and 'tatoes, and some roastin' ears.' By the time I'm ready to leave, she'll have my car filled up with corn and tomatoes and potatoes and anything else she has grown. And she'll say, 'Listen, Doc, we're agoin' to kill that big hog next week, and, boy, is he a fine one! And when we get it killed we're agoin' to give you a carve out o' it.' "

Gaine Cannon's eyes light up when he talks about his people. A few weeks ago, responding to a call from a mountain home, he discovered a small baby with a case of pneumonia.

"Penicillin wouldn't cure the infant quickly enough," he reports. "I told his father that he required hospitalization at once. The father said he had no money. But we got the baby to the hospital." Oxygen was required, and the doctor gave the parents a note to the hospital, saying he would stand for the bill, which he later paid. The baby recovered, and Gaine Cannon feels more than repaid what it cost him.

He remembers treating a baby several years ago. This little patient, too, had pneumonia. "She's in mighty bad shape," he told the parents as soon as he had given her a preliminary examination. "She may die tonight. But I believe penicillin will save her."

But he knew that he could not stay with the baby throughout the night because he had another desperately sick child in a community several miles away.

"You'll have to sit up with this baby," he told the parents, "and watch her carefully until I can get back. I can't stay; I've got another baby who's about to die and I've got to go look after her. But don't you let your baby go to sleep. Shake her, spank her, keep her conscious. And I'll be back as soon as I can."

He reached the bedside of the other child. "She's adyin' Doc," the mother said. "She's plumb stopped abreathin'."

By using mouth-to-mouth respiration he got the child to breathe again. The little girl was very low, however, and several times it was necessary for him to give artificial respiration, and on the way to the hospital some hours later they had to stop while he repeated it. But the little girl recovered. "Every time I go back to their home," he says, "the mother says to that child, 'This is the doctor who saved your life.' And that gives me a wonderful feeling."

When Dr. Cannon returned to the first baby, he found the infant much better. The penicillin had been successful. "She died three times while you was gone," the father reported, "but ever' time she died I spanked her and she come back to life."

Once again Gaine Cannon considered himself well paid for his services.

"I love these people. They're my folk," he repeats. "I undersand them and appreciate them, and I believe they understand and appreciate me. At any rate, I have no higher hope than to continue to live here at Balsam Grove and operate the little hospital we'll soon have and do the best I can to soothe their pains and restore their health—to share with them a proper reverence for life."

He doesn't expect to be repaid in money, but sometimes he is agreeably surprised. "Some time ago I had a patient with an illness that baffled me," he says. "I wanted very much to discover what the illness was, and of course I also wanted the fellow to get well. So I made arrangements for him to be admitted to St. Francis Hospital, in Greenville. They found his trouble, treated him, and he was released. And though my income was modest—what mountain doctor's isn't?—I paid his bill. And do you know, as soon as he was able to work he got a job and started paying me back, and now he is almost paid up."

That this particular fellow was a moonshiner who back in the hills had made many a run of corn whiskey was of no concern to Gaine Cannon. "He valued his life just as much as the preacher valued his," he explains, "and I valued both, and equally, I'd say," he adds, grinning. "And my patients aren't long in sensing that, and their understanding it makes my job of treating their ailments easier."

There is an interesting sequel to the story of this moonshiner's hospitalization Gaine Cannon reveals.

"He came to see me a few weeks ago. 'Doc,' he said, 'I want to get some more of my stomach medicine—you know, my vomitin' medicine.' What he meant was medicine to keep him from vomiting. 'I've got me a job in New York City with a man who's collecting ivy,' he explained, 'and I don't want to take no chanct o' runnin' out o' my medicine while I'm up there. He's agoin' to pay me seventy dollars a week.'

"The people around here call mountain laurel 'ivy,'" Dr. Cannon explains. They collect it, and also moss, and sell it for use in funerals, as wreaths and sprays, and for other decorative purposes. Often you can go to a mountain home and ask for the man of the house, and you'll be told he's away in the mountains, gathering ivy. Only they don't express it that way. The other day, for instance, I went over to Cannon McCall's house. But only Aunt Corrie was there. 'Aunt Corrie, where are Cannon and the boys this morning?' I asked.

" 'Well now, Doc,' she answered as she brushed a wisp of gray hair from her forehead with the back of her hand, 'they're out abreakin' ivy. I reckon they'll be a comin' back 'fore too long.' "

Gathering mountain laurel and rhododendron leaves and the

interesting leaves of the galax plant, another evergreen used extensively in making funeral decorations, provides some mountain families with most of the cash income they receive. And when an otherwise unemployed mountaineer gets a job paying him seventy dollars a week, like the one who was hired by the New Yorker, perhaps to help with the processing of the leaves, he considers himself a member of the wealthy citizenship. And by Balsam Grove standards, the doctor adds, he is.

"But in heart and soul he's still a mountaineer," Gaine Cannon insists. "It's characteristic of them that they may go off somewhere to a good job and work until they have saved up a little money, and then they come straight as a martin to its gourd right back to the little cove or hillside cabin they have left. It's funny how these people who buy the evergreen leaves—our folk call them 'ivy men'—come down here, and others come up from Florida, and become attached to these mountaineers and want to do something for them. So sometimes they offer them jobs, like this fellow who offered the Balsam Grove man the job in New York, and now and then they accept.

"Usually in a few months, maybe weeks, they're back, however, breaking ivy and probably on relief. I'm expecting this fellow back from New York any day now. He'll come in and tell me he had to come home. 'Now, Doc,' he'll say, 'I just plumb run out o' that there vomitin' medicine you give me, and I couldn't find no more up there, so I just come on home.' And he'll be out in the mountains, breaking ivy, and back on the welfare rolls in Brevard."

Gaine Cannon naturally knows who is on welfare. This man who got the New York job is an example.

"He was on welfare, and he was a mighty sick man, as the

specialists at the hospital in Greenville would discover after I sent him down there," Dr. Cannon reviews his case history. "He had had a fallen kidney on one side; he'd had an ulcer of the stomach, and a prostate disorder. The welfare people insisted that he see a doctor in Brevard. He told me about it when he came to our clinic.

" 'You've got to go to a doctor here in Brevard and let him examine you,' " the welfare folk said to him. " 'We'll have to have his report before we can do anything for you.' "

" 'What do you mean, another doctor?' " he asked. " 'You mean I can't go to *my* doctor, Dr. Cannon?' "

" 'We have to have two doctors' say-so about this,' " he was told. " 'So you'll have to have another doctor examine you.' "

" 'That's all right, then,' " my moonshiner friend agreed. " 'I'll go and see one, but I ain't agoin' to give up my doctor, over't Balsam Grove.' "

"He did go to another doctor, who had never seen him before and was, of course, not acquainted with his history. So this other doctor examined him by taking his blood pressure and listening to his heartbeat. 'You're all right,' he reported. 'Nothing wrong with you. You can go to work.' "

The welfare folk were sitting for him when he came in. "You're able to work. The doctor says you are."

"Yeh," said Gaine Cannon's patient, "the doctor over here says that, but I'm agoin' to go by what *my* doctor says. He knows my case. He knows what they done to me in the hospital down at Greenville. He's got the records and the X rays 'bout me. When he tells me I'm able to go to work, I'll try it. But right now I can't make it 'cause every day or two I dang nigh puke my head off."

"And he's right, he does," Gaine Cannon agrees. "He has

a difficult time retaining his food. I've been treating him for it. I give him inoculations in the veins, in the muscles, and medicine to take. Now and then he's able to go back to breaking ivy and making a little money. But not for long. And he won't be long on that job in New York. I consider the man totally disabled, and I do all I can to get the welfare people to help him.

"Those welfare folk over at Brevard have the idea that I lean over to help these people get welfare aid," Dr. Cannon says. "Well, I do. I think the patient needs it more than the welfare department, which is supported by the citizens, of course. So if folk come to me sick and unable to work, I try to help them. And in cases where there is doubt, I generally give them the benefit of the doubt. I often say to such a patient, 'Now you ought to go over to Brevard and let another doctor look at you too.' And most of the time the patient will look at me with a wry grin. 'Doc, now I ain't agoin' to do that,' he'll declare. "I'm astickin' to you, Doc.' "

So Gaine Cannon is sometimes at variance with the welfare people over at Brevard as well as other agencies whose purpose is to provide aid.

"Now and then we have to oppose something they are proposing to do or try to push them into doing something they don't want to do," Dr. Cannon reveals. "When we do have these disagreements, it is invariably because—they say this, and I agree it's true—I am trying to get more for the poor man or woman or child applying to them for help. Sometimes our fight is with the welfare people, sometimes the government, sometimes the rehabilitation folk. Not with the purposes and principles of these organizations, of course, but sometimes with the administration of these agencies. I have always seen red when 'red tape' has entangled a situation

[165]

and prevented or delayed the accomplishment of something that reason and common sense showed plainly should be done."

To illustrate he tells of the experience of one of his patients. This man had a spinal disorder that caused him to walk with his upper torso almost parallel to the ground. He came to the notice of the rehabilitation organization, and they sent him down to the Baptist Hospital, at Winston-Salem, for an operation that straightened him up; they paid for two or three trips down there and back for examinations and checkups. Then before he was rehabilitated to the point where he could go to work and begin earning his way, Dr. Cannon says, they cut him off. "From now on," they told him, "you'll have to furnish your own transportation to and from the hospital. We haven't any more money to spend on your case."

"I contend that is poor business," Gaine Cannon insists. "They have him almost to the place where he can go to work and begin earning his way, and then they stop helping him. He still has to go back to Winston-Salem for treatments, and there and back, that's two hundred miles. And it's only because of the goodness of these mountain folk that he is able to make those trips. They provide transportation.

"That same procedure has been followed in other cases," Dr. Cannon says. "For instance, if a man needs an appendectomy, they will supply it. But often they don't follow it up with needed care. I maintain that if they start something, even if it costs five hundred or a thousand dollars, they should see the thing through, and not go just so far and then stop. I have all due respect for the welfare and rehabilitation programs, but I feel that they should not lose interest in a case or stop support of it in the middle of the treatment. But I don't want to be unfair. I admit that I am always likely to be prejudiced, when there's a conflict between the organization and the individual, on the side of the individual. Life is not in things, in organizations, however good they may be, however dedicated to good works they may be. Life is in the individual—man, animal, insect."

CHAPTER
14

From the first days since Gaine Cannon moved into the farmhouse in the cove through which Shoal Creek meanders, his program of service to the Balsam Grove community has been continually enlarging, and so has the area of the region he has been serving. But he has been looking ahead hopefully to the completion of the hospital named for Albert Schweitzer, whose life and philosophy have so powerfully shaped the course of his action and thinking.

He sees in the small facility at Balsam Grove an instrument for the realization of the Schweitzer philosophy in an expanding neighorhood moving into a new economy and a materially altered pattern of living. As he has been observing these changing modes in the mountains and helping to hasten some of them, he has become more confirmed in his devotion to Dr. Schweitzer and his philosophy.

But the clinic in the little farmhouse and the obstetrics building developed from the old two-car garage had been in use seven years and the sturdy stone-faced walls of the hospital were nearing completion before he would have an opportunity personally to meet Albert Schweitzer. It was in January 1961 when they first met. They stood on the dock at the little boat landing at Lambaréné. For Gaine Cannon the meeting was one of the most thrilling moments of his life. He would never tire of recounting his visit to Dr. Schweitzer in his sprawling hospital in French Equatorial Africa and working there with him and members of his staff.

"One day early in 1960, I was in a friend's office over in Brevard when the telephone rang and the long-distance operator asked if I was there," he recalls. "When I was put on the line, a voice inquired, 'Is this Dr. Cannon of the Albert Schweitzer Memorial Hospital?' I said it was. 'Well, at last I've caught the mystery man!' the pleasant voice exclaimed. Then the man introduced himself:

" 'Dr. Cannon, this is Dr. Phillips, in Chicago. I'm a dentist here, and I'm president of the Albert Schweitzer Education Foundation, which is an organization whose purpose is to promote the spread throughout the world of an understanding and appreciation of Dr. Schweitzer's philosophy. We have been intrigued to discover that a hospital in the North Carolina mountains has been named for Dr. Schweitzer. We figured that you must be a great admirer of the doctor's and that you, too, are interested in the dissemination of his ideas.

" 'Well, we are having here in Chicago a meeting of what we are calling the First Congress of Albert Schweitzer Scholars. We will meet for a week' (he gave the dates) 'for the purpose of translating Dr. Schweitzer's philosophy from German into simple, everyday English so that everyone can understand it. We want to spread everywhere an understanding of his reverence for life, and we believe that if we can do this we will be able to hasten the ending of war. Our foundation would like to see reverence for life taught in the schools, in the Sunday schools, from the pulpits; we would like to see professorships of philosophy established in the various colleges and universities for the teaching of Albert Schweitzer's philosophy. But I'm calling you, Doctor, to ask if you will come to Chicago and join us for this session. If you can't get away for the week, maybe you could come for the last three days.'

" 'Dr. Phillips, if it's anything concerning Dr. Schweitzer,' I answered, 'I'll come for the entire week.' He told me he was glad I could come. And I said that I would do anything I could to promote the project. 'But, Dr. Phillips,' I asked, 'how did you hear of me and our little hospital?' "

Dr. Phillips replied that he had seen an article in a newspaper about Dr. Cannon's work and his interest in Dr. Schweitzer, and he had been trying to reach Dr. Cannon on the telephone, but since there was no line to the hospital, he had been having difficulty locating him.

Gaine Cannon went to Chicago leaving his assistant Dr. Clarence Edens in charge at the clinic. He found scholars there from every section of the country, and one man from Switzerland. The group of about twenty-five persons included professors of philosophy in various colleges and universities in the United States and presidents of such institutions, several of whom had won prizes for writing essays on Albert Schweitzer. Dr. Cannon was the only doctor of medicine in the group. While the Schweitzer enthusiasts were engaged in discussing the Schweitzer philosophy and translating it from the German into simple, understandable English, they had as guests several Nobel Prize winners who happened to be meeting in Chicago that week.

The group also discussed plans to visit Dr. Schweitzer and present to him the translation they were making of his writings. The translators wanted his approval of their work before they made arrangements for printing and distributing it.

The original plan decided upon was to go to Lambaréné early in 1962, but later the date was advanced a year.

The party started from New York on December 27, 1960, the day after Gaine Cannon had left Balsam Grove, once again trusting Dr. Edens to run the clinic, and flew by jet to London, where they arrived in a little more than five hours. There the travelers stayed two days and met several notables, including Charles Galton Darwin and historian Arnold Toynbee, with whom the visitors had dinner and discussed the mission to Lambaréné. Dr. Cannon tells of the group and its further traveling.

"The delegation was composed of thirteen of the people who had met in Chicago and one Schweitzer enthusiast from Ireland. This man from Ireland joined us in London; he had written one of the first books on Dr. Schweitzer's amazing career. Three ladies were in the party, one a Chinese doctor of philosophy and another an American doctor of philosophy. The American was a German scholar and spoke the language fluently. Again I was the only doctor of medicine.

"From London we flew to Paris. Dr. Schweitzer's daughter Rhena came from her home in Switzerland to have dinner with us that evening and breakfast the next morning. After talking with her about her famous father and his philosophy, we left in the evening for Douala, Africa, four thousand miles away and almost straight south. We took off from Paris between nine and ten o'clock, and the next morning landed at Douala, in the French Cameroons. A DC-4, an old American plane, picked us up there for the last leg of the flight. They call these planes 'milk hoppers' because they hop from one settlement to another, carrying freight, most of it foods of various kinds; they unload shipments and pick up others for delivery to communities farther on. But finally our plane came down at Lambaréné.

"Two jeeps were waiting. They took us and our baggage down to the Ogowe River, where we were put on a motor launch and started across the great stream toward Dr. Schweitzer's hospital. There was no road into the hospital grounds, the drivers explained, and the only way to reach it was by boat. And still we were a long way from our destination.

"The Ogowe is a huge river. It reminded me of the Mississippi, which I'd seen some years before. Because there was a considerable current, we had to push upstream a little in order to land where we wished on the other side, and it took us about forty minutes.

"They say the world stands still at Lambaréné. There it is little changed—it must be—since time began. Lambaréné drowses beside the great river near the converging of several streams, the throughways of Africa, and all about is the jungle, dark, mysterious, impenetrable, dangerous. Flowers gorgeous in shape and coloring push down to the Ogowe's banks and fade away into the swamp grasses. Parrots sail fan-tailed above the water's edge, and monkeys from their palm tree perches chatter like gossiping housewives. Here and there in the shallow muck stands a stork, his head sideways and his beady eyes searching for an unwary small fish. And above all is the sky, cloudless and still. I had the feeling, as we approached the other bank of the Ogowe, that this was the way it had been on the river the morning after creation, whenever and however that was.

"Timeless. Unchanging. Serene, unruffled, under a blazing sun or the dark of the moon, always the same. Unmoving, except for the parrots and the monkeys and the small waves stirred by our boat, and yet underneath the calm and the unstirring timelessness a seething convolution of life, an endless battling for life and against life in every form—insects, the malarial mosquito, the tsetse fly carrying sleeping sickness, ants, snakes, fish, myriad animals and birds of the jungle, innumerable black men, Pygmies and erect, tall, handsome, bronzed fellows, cannibals, fierce fighters, and intelligent, gentle, courteous, and kindly folk."

Westward, beyond the teeming swamps and the equatorial heat, beyond a wide ocean and other swamps and flatlands and rolling hills, Gaine Cannon saw in his mind's eye a familiar land of cooling breezes and sometimes deep snows, but serene, too, and unharried, and peopled with kindly and courteous folk.

"I thought of our Blue Ridge Mountains and our Great Smokies. Rock-ribbed, enduring, eternal in their fierce upthrust, sleeping away the days in the silence of a wide solitude, though sometimes troubled and lashed in the quick frenzy of a mountain storm. I thought of the life in our hills: the teeming, burgeoning life, the fish in our little creek sweeping under the wooden bridge with the cowbars and around the bend beneath the apple tree and past the old farmhouse and through the curving of the narrow channel in front of the hospital building, and countless birds and worms and bees and howling dogs and wildcats that scream and snarl in the night, and foxes and coons and cows and mules (for we still use mules in the mountains) and the people, my wonderful folk of the highlands and the huddled coves, the valleys and the steep slopes, changeless, too, I hoped, in their sturdiness, their inborn civility and good-naturedness, changeless though changing.

"And I pondered why I had come to Africa. Was it not to

learn more about this reverence for life, this aversion to destroying something one cannot create, something one can never bestow?

"Then someone exclaimed and pointed. And I saw *him*.

"He was standing on the small landing dock, watching us approach. He was a large man, I saw, somewhat stocky and slightly stooped, though not much for a man who in a few days, on January 14, would be eighty-six. A sun helmet covered with white cloth was pushed back on his head, to reveal a square, full face framing a drooping, scraggly mustache. He was wearing a white shirt, open at the throat, with sleeves cut off at the elbows. His trousers were khaki, and when afterward I stood beside him I saw that in places they were patched.

"But I was little concerned with the cut or color of his trousers or the patches on them. Or that his arms were muscular like a blacksmith's and that he was tanned to the color of old leather. I was hardly aware of anything except that here, at last, I was looking across the fast narrowing water of a great African river to a small landing pier on which I saw standing, in the simplicity and sincerity of my old mountain-doctor father, the man I had come to venerate as the greatest man, save Jesus Christ, of all time.

"Reverence for life, fierce hostility to everything and every concept that would bring trouble and pain needlessly to any of God's creatures. I was looking at the idea incarnate, the principle personified. And as our launch pushed up to the landing place, I thought again of the saying of the Galilean: 'I am come that they might have life, and have it more abundantly.' The idea struck me that I myself had come to the best place in all the world in which to begin to learn the meaning of those immortal words."

CHAPTER

15

DR. SCHWEITZER didn't greet anyone until everybody was off
the launch and all the baggage had been set out. Then he
began shaking hands. Some in the group he knew already,
and these he kissed on each cheek and patted on the shoulder.
Then he pointed along the wide path that led to the hospital,
and bending down, picked up a suitcase in each hand and
started trudging up the hill. Each visitor picked up his own
luggage and fell in behind the doctor. All had been warned
not to protest at Dr. Schweitzer's carrying the bags. If anyone should, it was suggested, the doctor would probably tell
him to mind his own business.

So the host led his visitors up to the quarters they would
occupy, and they began to acquaint themselves with
the place. A little later each guest was assigned his share of the
work. Gaine Cannon soon found that everyone who visits the
hospital must work half of each day, if he is physically able,
and there are many kinds of jobs. The status of a man or
woman in the world beyond Lambaréné does not affect the
assignment he is given. Some work in the hospital; others, like

[175]

the philosophers, for example, work on the grounds, tending the garden patches, building roads and bridges, and filling in places washed out by the region's torrential rains. One of the professors in the group from the United States was in the gang that shoveled dirt and loaded and pushed wheelbarrows. The women worked too; their assignment was in the nursery, changing and feeding the babies.

Shortly after the American party arrived, they were joined by an American woman who had been coming to Lambaréné each year for Dr. Schweitzer's birthday anniversary. She was a doctor of philosophy and a doctor of music. She and Gaine Cannon quickly became friends, and shortly she would be one of the most faithful and enthusiastic supporters of his hospital project at Balsam Grove. Dr. Cannon tells about her:

"She is Dr. Marion Mill Preminger, a great friend of the African people. She's a world traveler, philosopher, author of a book, *The Sands of Tamanrasset*, which received the Christopher Award, and last year became the only non-African recipient from President M'Ba of Gabon of the Grand Officer of the Equatorial Star and Grand Medal of the Gabon Renaissance. But more important, to me, at any rate, she is a devoted follower of Albert Schweitzer, who has contributed generously and with enthusiasm to his great work. She has visited him on his birthday every year for the last eleven years. She goes to his birthday observance and stays two or three months in the leper colony there. Many persons who know of her devotion to Dr. Schweitzer, his philosophy, and his work perhaps wonder how she became so interested in him. The story she told me was that she was on a plane one day—it was in this country—and a diabetic on the plane with her had forgotten to bring along his insulin and had a reaction. She took care of him in the emergency and probably saved his life. She got the plane to land and took him off, brought him to a hospital, and looked after him until the emergency was past. Fortunately for her, this man was a friend of Dr. Schweitzer's. He gave her a letter of introduction to the doctor. And through that letter Dr. Schweitzer invited her to come to Africa. Had it not been for the letter, she told me, he probably would never have seen her, for generally, she said, the doctor doesn't take much stock in actors and dancers, and she was both. But she did visit him and they became devoted friends. It has been estimated that Dr. Preminger has raised perhaps a million dollars for the hospital at Lambaréné by giving lectures throughout the United States on Schweitzer and his work and by soliciting contributions from her friends throughout the Western world."

Gaine Cannon's assignment at Lambaréné was in the operating room. It happened that just as the American group was arriving, the hospital temporarily lost one of its surgeons. So Dr. Cannon was handed a gown, rubber gloves, and a cap and mask and asked to take the place of the absent staff member.

"It was a moving experience to find myself on the equator in Africa's steaming jungles, working as skillfully as I could to bring relief and healing to poor black men lying helpless but trusting under my hands," Gaine Cannon said later of this service at Lambaréné. "But how can I ever describe the way I felt, realizing that beside me, his heart and brain and strong sunburned hands bent on replenishing and strengthening in these little ones among God's children the flickering flame of life, stood one of the world's greatest citizens!

"I hadn't found him in any of the world capitals or presiding on the dais in the assembly hall of the United Nations. I hadn't found him wearing the frock coat and striped trousers of the statesman or the bemedaled uniform of the commanding general. I had found him inside the crude compound of a jungle hospital, perspiration pouring down his cheeks."

Many visitors to Lambaréné on their return home have described the Schweitzer hospital and its staff and the ever present horde of patients, their families, and their innumerable pets. Some stress one phase of the place and its work, others see the hospital and the people in another light. Gaine Cannon, returned to Balsam Grove and the routine of mountain practice, delights in revealing his version of Lambaréné.

"The main hospital building is at the head of the path from the hospital landing place. Here the path joins a road that swings around to the right and splits into several ways that serve the staff area between the hospital landing and a couple of hunded yards farther along the river the landing place for the dwelling houses. Beyond this area and lying on the riverside are the garden areas. I was surprised to discover that Dr. Schweitzer's hospital compound is comprised of between forty and fifty buildings, some of them very small, most of them sheltered and almost hidden beneath the palms and the okoumes. Only this shade, I'm quite sure, makes the buildings endurable, particularly to Europeans and Americans, for even under the trees the heat here on the equator is terrific. I was surprised, too, to learn that this hospital serves perhaps a thousand persons a day. This number, however, includes many members of the patients' families, for in French Equatorial Africa when someone goes to the hospital for treatment his family goes along. Usually the wife accompanies her husband to do his cooking; he would be unwilling to eat anyone else's cooking for fear he would be poisoned."

Despite Dr. Cannon's experience in American hospitals and in the Army, he was unprepared for the motley character of the assemblage at Dr. Schweitzer's hospital.

"We found at Lambaréné some thousand persons," he reveals, "including patients and their relatives and the hospital staff, of whom about three hundred and fifty were patients in varying stages of leprosy, and a menagerie impossible to estimate and of all descriptions, not only running about the hospital grounds but through the buildings—monkeys, goats, dogs, chickens, cats, pigeons, parrots, a few pelicans, one of which at six o'clock each evening flies up from the river and sits above the stairway to Dr. Schweitzer's room; there he stays, guarding the doctor until daylight, when he returns to the river to look for fish.

"I confess that even though I had read about the animals at Lambaréné and had agreed heartily with Dr. Schweitzer in his philosophy of reverence for life, I was shocked when I saw goats, dogs, cats, and other animals and fowl running through the wards and among the patients, some of whom were critically ill. It did violence to my years of training and working in modern hospitals. 'Why does Dr. Schweitzer permit this?' many persons have asked me since my return from Lambaréné. 'Surely he is a modern and skillful physician who understands about germs and contagion.'

"He does, of course. And his reverence for life doesn't forbid his killing germs. Many persons who have read about him have an exaggerated idea about his philosophy. I have heard people say that Dr. Schweitzer would kill nothing. This isn't true. He says that one must destroy some forms of life, poisonous snakes, for example, for the sake of higher forms. But he does insist that one should not destroy life unnecessarily. He bitterly decries such activities as the killing of wild animals for so-called sport."

At Lambaréné, however, Dr. Cannon learned that it was not only because Dr. Schweitzer believes in saving rather than destroying life that he permits animals and that even more dangerous animal from a health standpoint, man, to roam at will about the hospital grounds and through the buildings, though he does insist on keeping them out of the operating room, perhaps the only sterile place in all Lambaréné.

"I discovered, strange to me at first though it does make sense, that Dr. Schweitzer allows this situation to exist also because he is convinced that the presence of the dogs and monkeys and birds has a good psychological effect upon the patients, that tends to hasten their recovery.

"Dr. Schweitzer says that if he built a modern hospital and operated it as hospitals in this country are operated, he wouldn't have the patients in the first place. They simply wouldn't come. The French Government has a modern hospital nearby, and it is half empty most of the time, he points out, despite the great need of additional hospital facilities in that region of Africa. And most of the patients the French hospital does have are white persons: missionaries, people in that region engaged in the lumber business, or commercial folk, and a few educated Africans.

"A sick man would refuse to go to the hospital, Dr. Schweitzer and his staff people told us, if he couldn't take his children, his goats, his dog, and perhaps his brothers and sisters, several of them, at any rate, and of course his wife to cook for him and wait on him. Sometimes patients with their strange entourages come from as far away as two hundred miles up the Ogowe River; they actually move to Lambaréné and squat down. They bring some rough mats, if they have them, and put these on the dirt floor beside the patient's bed. Sometimes they bring a little food, but more often they subsist on what the hospital supplies. But they cook their own food because of their fear of being poisoned by an enemy. So the hospital gives them the raw food, bananas and breadfruit and such staples, and they cook it in their little pots right there on the hospital grounds, perhaps as near the patient as they can build their fires. They set the pots on pebbles and collect sticks and leaves for fuel.

"You can go along what they call Hospital Street, which is just a little graveled way with holes and ups and downs in it, not a street at all as we term it, and you'll see dozens of tiny fires over which they are cooking. They sit there hunkered down over the pots, stirring the bubbling mixtures, and they serve their sick folk and then eat the same fare."

So throughout the great hospital compound at Lambaréné, Dr. Cannon and the others of the visiting delegation found these innumerable small worlds to themselves, each a patient and his family, his relatives and pets.

"If a patient is coming two hunded miles for treatment, probably a major operation, he is in fact moving," Dr. Cannon says. "He brings all his possessions with him. He doesn't know whether he is going back, so he brings with him everything he has of any value. Invariably he brings his pets. And soon his pets are multiplying all over the place. And in the midst of it, bestowing his service and his sympathy and his love upon them all, moves Dr. Schweitzer. Sometimes dogs fight and are injured; Dr. Schweitzer treats each dog just as he has been treating the dog's owner, or even if he has no owner. The hospital is truly an amazing institution.

"In the middle of the night—it happened several times while we were there—you may hear a bell ringing and then much scurrying through the building and along the paths under the trees. The ringing of the bell announces that an emergency has arisen. Maybe one of the patients must have a sudden operation, and help is being summoned. But maybe an animal has been injured; he, too, must have emergency

[181]

treatment. And he gets it. I wonder how many times the doctor has been roused from sound slumber to set a broken leg for a dog or cat."

To serve this mass of people and animals, the visitors to Lambaréné discovered, was a staff, exclusive of Dr. Schweitzer, of only five doctors, including the one who was away at the time, so that Dr. Cannon made the fifth. One was Japanese; the others were German and Swiss. The Japanese doctor looked after the lepers.

"At Lambaréné, they told us, they customarily operate three or four days a week, and they try to keep two surgical teams busy at the same time, although they have but one operating room. They accomplish this by having two operating tables in that room. While our group was there, one of the staff doctors and I composed a team. I assisted him on several interesting operations; they have a wide variety to do at Lambaréné, including many types of hernia."

The most unusual operation to Dr. Cannon was one that is frequently performed, though he had never before seen it. The ailment that necessitates this operation is as far removed from the North Carolina mountains as any could be, for it is endemic in tropical regions. The disease is known as elephantiasis; the victim's limb becomes enormously enlarged and the skin is thick, hard, and grooved like an elephant's hide. It is caused by a parasitic worm that infests the affected part. Dr. Cannon relates his experience.

"I was certain that my colleague, Dr. Rolf Müller of Switzerland, would amputate the man's leg when we prepared to operate on the first case of elephantiasis in which I assisted. The leg was huge; it was a terrible-looking thing, and I saw no possibility of saving it. But the doctor seemed little perturbed, for the case, I would soon learn, was a routine one; he had done many elephantiasis operations.

"When the patient had been anesthetized, the doctor made a long incision in the leg, and I knew then that he was not contemplating amputation. He just made this long incision, and then methodically began peeling away the extra growth on the outside of the bone. It was a remarkable operation for me to watch, and to have a very minor part in. The extra growth in the soft tissue is caused by what is called a filaria parasite. He cut and scraped all this out right down to the tendons and muscles and bone, and when he had finished the leg was down to normal size and matched the patient's other, which I noticed had previously been operated on for a similar ailment. Soon this fellow was walking around on it without difficulty.

"I learned from Dr. Schweitzer and his colleagues that many Africans suffer from infestations of various parasites. And I saw a number of cases in which these parasites had gained footholds in unfortunate victims. But one of the strangest was that of a fellow who came in one day with something wrong with an eye. I'd never seen anything like it.

"One of these filaria had attached itself under the covering of his eye and had grown so large that it had the eyelid jumping. The doctor dropped a little novocain in the man's eye and made a small incision. Then with a tiny forceps he pulled the thing out. It must have been two inches long and it was wriggling and twisting like a snake; in fact, that's what it looked like, a tiny snake. It was a ghastly-looking thing: I had never seen anything like it in all my medical training and practice. When the surgeon cut into the eye covering, the filaria, a different type from the one that causes elephantiasis, was curled up just like a snake ready to strike.

[183]

"The surgeon, I might point out, had no reverence for the filaria's life. He very quickly disposed of it. No doubt Dr. Schweitzer himself has killed many."

In the operating room, Dr. Cannon would discover, surgeons wear the usual gowns, masks, and caps, but while they are on duty at other times they wear aprons that look very much like the aprons worn by American carpenters; the aprons have bibs that cover the chest and loop around the neck; they go down about to the knees and have pockets in them in which the doctors carry instruments and medicines. At Lambaréné, unlike Balsam Grove, he would also learn, the doctors do not visit the patients unless they are too ill to come to the doctor. The hospital has sick calls, very much as in the Army, and patients who are able to walk swarm out of the wards and come to the doctor. Sometimes, he learned, there may be a hundred patients lined up at one time, waiting their turn to have the doctor examine them. And sometimes the conduct of the doctors at Lambaréné, to American and European physicians, must appear almost as unorthodox as that of their patients. Dr. Cannon gives an example:

"I remember that Dr. Müller, with whom I was working, one day had a tiny baby monkey, probably only four or five days old, that he had wrapped in a sheet of cellophane and was carrying in one of the pockets of his apron. I was with him some ten days, and he carried the little monkey most of that time; in that short period the monkey developed both in size and intelligence. He was a mischievous little fellow, too; one day I saw him reach up slyly and grab the doctor's pencil and put it down into the pocket.

"No one thought it unusual for the doctor to be carrying the little monkey with him while he went about his duties. You see people taking bits of food away from the dining room when they have finished their meals; the scraps are for their pets." He learned how there happened to be so many goats at Lambaréné.

"Some wealthy man, they told us, had got the idea that Dr. Schweitzer should raise goats so that the hospital might have an abundance of fresh milk. The doctor told him that the goats wouldn't give milk there, that the climate was too hot. But the rich friend persisted. He even had the goats kept for a while in some other hot region in the hope that they might become acclimated. Then he sent them to Dr. Schweitzer. But the goats, although they would reproduce, would not give enough milk; they gave hardly enough to raise their own off-spring. I saw patients sitting around feeding tiny goats from bottles with nipples on them; perhaps the formulas were the same as those used for babies."

Milk has to be brought in to Lambaréné, Dr. Cannon's group was told. At the hospital they use powdered milk sent in from various countries by friends of Dr. Schweitzer's. While the party was there, he recalls, a birthday present for Dr. Schweitzer arrived from the United States. It was eighty-six *tons* of medicines and supplies, one ton for each year of his age. The day it arrived, Dr. Cannon watched him down at the landing, supervising the boys who were unloading these welcome drugs and other needed supplies from the boat and rolling them in wheelbarrows up to the hospital's storage room. They were jumping to the doctor's commands. Albert Schweitzer, everyone at Lambaréné knows, is head man at the hospital. And certainly no one challenges him to prove it. "I am your brother," he tells the natives, "but your *elder* brother."

"Dr. Schweitzer keeps a constant and close watch on the room where he stores drugs and other pharmaceutical supplies," Dr. Cannon says. "Because of the terrific heat and humidity of the Gabon region, he must keep his medicines in containers that dampness will not affect, such as metal boxes and glass bottles. And these supplies are so precious that they must at all times be carefully rationed and allotted to only the neediest cases. He is never sure that the hospital won't use up all its supplies of this sort before new shipments are available."

Albert Schweitzer is indeed head man at Lambaréné and elder brother to anyone who visits the hospital, whether he is a black man from up the Ogowe or a personage from America or Europe. Members of the group from the United States were told the story, for example, that when Adlai Stevenson was visiting the doctor he suddenly slapped a mosquito that had alighted either on his shoulder or Dr. Schweitzer's.

"I'll have you to know," exclaimed Mr. Stevenson's host, "that was my mosquito you killed!" And he shook a finger at his famous guest, who wasn't sure that Dr. Schweitzer was joking. Nor was Gaine Cannon when he heard the story.

"I'm quite sure, though," Dr. Cannon reiterates, "that Dr. Schweitzer's reverence for life does not go so far as to cause him to oppose the destruction of such harmful insects as malaria-bearing mosquitoes. But he doesn't countenance the killing of any strays around the hospital, and consequently dogs and cats, monkeys, goats, pigeons, breeding all the time, fairly swarm over the compound. Some of them looked to me like they would have been better off dead, they were so thin and emaciated. But I heard that somebody made that observation to Dr. Schweitzer and asked him if he didn't think so too. 'Ask the Man who created them,' he is reported to have said. 'Let Him say.'"

Many stories are told about Dr. Schweitzer to illustrate his hatred of killing, and he himself tells some good ones. One day he related to the American visitors an account of a farmer—he may have lived in the Gabon district—whose cat ate the farmer's pet rabbit. The man was very angry. He put the cat in a bag and tied it securely; then he carried the cat in the bag to a creek nearby and threw cat and bag in. Later that evening there was a scratching at the farmer's door, and when he opened it, there were the cat and the farmer's dog. The dog had followed the farmer to the creek, pulled out the bag, and released the cat. The poor dumb animal, Dr. Schweitzer declared, had shown more kindness than the man.

The group of which Dr. Cannon was a member heard an amusing story that involved Dr. Schweitzer's daughter, Rhena Eckart. She customarily works six months in Africa with her father and spends the other six months of the year with her husband and family at their home in Switzerland. Once while she was in Africa she became considerably annoyed. "Father, if you don't do something to get rid of those rats," she declared, "I'm going to have to leave."

"Daughter," her father replied, "we're going to miss you."

They tell another story of Dr. Schweitzer and rats. This day he had gone up the river to investigate some construction being done there. While he was away, Mrs. Schweitzer had instructed some native boys to catch rats, which had been giving them much trouble and annoyance; she instructed the boys to put the rats in a sack and carry them up the river a mile or two and drown them.

The boys caught the rats, put them into the sack, and started up the river. But hardly had they got beyond the hospital compound when they met Dr. Schweitzer returning.

"What have you in that bag, boys?" he asked.

They told him they had rats that the doctor's wife had ordered them to catch.

"And what were you going to do with them?" he asked, although he was fairly certain he knew.

They said his wife had instructed them to throw the bag and rats into the river.

"Yes, I understand," Dr. Schweitzer said, reaching for the bag. "Just give them to me, and you boys go on back to the hospital. I'll attend to this."

He did. He took the sack over beside the river, but he did not throw it in; he opened it instead and let the rats out. The rats, the story goes, were back at the hospital before the doctor was.

Many persons, Dr. Cannon says, wonder why in a hot country with all those rats and pets and people, and with sanitary conditions never good, disease is not rampant, why the people do not die literally like flies.

"In fact, I wonder myself," he confides. "I suppose the answer is that the people build up an immunity. I was interested in checking the records at the hospital on post-operative infections; I found that their records were as good as ours in the United States, perhaps better. One would expect that with their lack of sanitation they would have an extremely high rate of post-operative infections, but they don't. And the sanitary conditions, compared with those prevailing in the most isolated areas even of our mountains, are fearful."

Dr. Cannon goes on more specifically to describe these conditions at the hospital at Lambaréné.

"In this great compound in which perhaps a thousand persons are treated daily and the patients' families live also, there is not a single indoor toilet; certainly I saw none. To dispose of the body wastes they use pots, which they empty into the river. For those able to use them, there are outside privies. Few Americans of our day, I suspect, have seen anything like them. One without particularly sensitive olfactory equipment can smell them a hundred yards off, and I was amazed to discover some privies not far from hospital buildings.

"Bathing facilities were almost as crude. They had set up a barrel with holes in it on a sort of stilt arrangement, and in the interest of modesty had placed some sheets of tin around these poles to provide a small enclosed place. A wood stove heated the water. When the water had become sufficiently hot, you undressed and lathered yourself with soap. Then you quickly poured the water into the barrel and ran under it; if you didn't hurry, all the water would run out before you got the suds rinsed off. From the outside of this shower bath you could see the feet of the bather. It reminded me of the little places along the curbs on Paris sidewalks, even though the use was different."

But the arrangements for the surgeons to scrub before beginning an operation looked just as ingenious to Dr. Cannon.

"They had set a barrel up on the wall, with a petcock at the bottom, into which they poured hot water. When the operating surgeons were ready, a little boy would turn the petcock so that the water flowed out, and the surgeons stood there with brushes, scrubbing while the water streamed on their hands and arms. The boy's operating the petcock made it unnecessary for the surgeon to touch anything. It was effective, even though a far cry from the plumbing we have, where you turn the water on and off with your elbow or foot and squirt liquid soap on your hands by stepping on a valve. The water, having been boiled, is sterile, of course. But it seems very crude by modern standards.

"And in the midst of our scrubbing there sat Dr. Schweitzer at his desk, writing one moment and consulting with a doctor the next on some treatment problem the younger physician had come to ask about, including surgery, for although the doctor was no longer willing because of his age to take the risk of operating, he was always avilable for consultation. All the while, patients were running in for treatment and pills, and other medicines were being handed out and instructions being given with patients, doctors, nurses, attendants, workmen and animals everywhere. But Dr. Schweitzer, I observed, seemed never disturbed by the people or the animals; sometimes he'd turn his head to look out the window, eyes unblinking, as though oblivious of everything going on around him.

"They don't even have electric lights, except in the operating room. And the generator that provides current for that must have been used on Noah's Ark. The doctors only start it up when they need lights for an operation; the lights are likely to go off a couple of times during an operation, and then someone must hold a flashlight for the surgeon until he finishes or they get the generator working again.

"Yet despite the lack of modern facilities and the hardships under which the staff works, the hospital has a remarkable rate of cures," Dr. Cannon reiterates, "and the doctors and nurses serve loyally and sympathetically and show an amazing commitment to fulfilling their duties."

CHAPTER
16

BUT there was one phase of living at Dr. Schweitzer's hospital that the American doctor found particularly pleasant. This was mealtime. Not only was the food good, but Dr. Schweitzer's manner of conducting the meals made them significant and memorable to Dr. Cannon and the others.

At Lambaréné the staff eat much fish and other sea food, and it is well prepared, Dr. Cannon discovered. About the only meat is alligator tails. "We had some while I was there; it tasted good," Dr. Cannon reports. "They cook the meat pretty much as we do beef stew. In addition we had wonderful fruit dishes, salads of one kind or another, and excellent soup."

Natives, supervised by white persons, do the cooking for those natives whose relatives aren't there to cook for them. But most of the cooking for the whites is done by white persons and served by them. Most of the whites at Lambaréné are German or Swiss.

"When our group was there, they had sixteen white nurses, and there were about forty white persons working in the hospital. They all eat together, and it is most impressive. Everyone sits down when he comes into the dining hall and waits until Dr. Schweitzer arrives. Then the entire group stands up and sits down with the doctor, and he asks the blessing.

"The dining room is a long structure, built of a material that looks like stone or cement blocks; it's open on all sides and screened so that if there's any breeze stirring the diners receive the advantage of it. It's always hot, certainly it was when we were there, from 110 to 120 degrees in the shade, and to anyone who has been spending most of his time in recent years in the North Carolina mountains that is hot. The perspiration was always running down my face, back, all over me, and down into my shoes. I felt sticky all the time. It's hot during the night, too. I found the heat was one hardship at Lambaréné difficult for me to endure.

"After the blessing Dr. Schweitzer, who sits in the center on one side of the long table, reads a short passage from the Bible in German. Then everyone eats. After they have finished eating, the doctor again opens his Bible and in German reads another passage, which he then discusses in an expository way. After this he gets up from the table and walks over to a battered piano and begins to play. Anyone can see at first glance that the instrument is old. I learned that it was a sort of piano-organ combination that was given to him years ago by a friend in Paris. Some of the keys stick and some are past playing at all. But I didn't learn this from Dr. Schweitzer's performance. So skillful was his handling of the keyboard, in fact, that he did not hit false notes or strike unresponsive keys. I have an idea that no one else in the world could have got from it the music that Dr. Schweitzer did. Only a few weeks ago I heard that Dr. Schweitzer (eighty-eight years old) was still going strong; that his fingers were still lively. I shall never forget the thrill of seeing him, said by many authorities to be *the* world's foremost student of the works of Johann Sebastian Bach, sitting there on a beaten rough bench before a dilapidated piano-organ and fashioning from it marvelous music.

"There is a service of this kind at every meal, but it is longer and more impressive at the evening meal. The way Dr. Schweitzer explains what he reads from the Bible might not appeal to some church members in America, but to me his expositions were logical and satisfying, and inspiring."

Gaine Cannon was particularly impressed one evening when Dr. Schweitzer in the devotional period read the story told by Jesus of the Good Samaritan. One of the guests at the dinner was a Dr. Friedman, a Jewish physician who had escaped from Germany during the Hitler era. The doctor's entire family had been killed, but he had been able to evade the Nazi executioners and get to one of the countries of the Near East. There he was another displaced person, with no passport, no home, little money, and with no place to establish a new practice. Somehow Dr. Schweitzer heard of him and invited him to come to Lambaréné and work in the hospital.

"After Dr. Schweitzer had read the Scriptural account of the Good Samaritan and explained it in his own fashion, Dr. Friedman remained in the dining room with several members of our group and talked. Dr. Schweitzer had gone out, and soon our conversation centered upon him," Dr. Cannon reveals. "Dr. Friedman spoke excellent English, as well as German and French.

" 'Dr. Schweitzer had a special reason for reading the story of the Good Samaritan tonight,' said Dr. Friedman. 'The story as Jesus told it probably has a message different from that given it by the reader who doesn't take time to look for a deeper meaning than seems to appear on the surface. But consider this story: Here's a Jew, and he has been robbed. It was logical that Jesus would select a Jew for the man who had been held up and robbed, because the Jews had money, and they were high-minded and proud. And two other Jews, coming along the road, saw their beaten brother Jew, but they were likewise proud, and perhaps their business was pressing. Probably they didn't want to soil their fine robes with the dust and the blood of this other Jew, or maybe they were afraid they'd miss a good business deal if they dallied to help their brother. At any rate, they passed him by without helping him.

" 'Then along came a Samaritan, and surely he had no love for Jews. He wasn't supposed to have, anyway. The Samaritans and the Jews loathed each other; the Jews thought they were better than the Samaritans, that their blood was better. And one would have expected that any Samaritan coming along a road and discovering a Jew beaten up and robbed would be happy about it, at least inwardly, feeling that he had got what he had coming to him. He might have suspected, and hoped, that the robber was a Samaritan and had added many coins to his bag.

" 'But this Samaritan didn't think or act as he was supposed to. He didn't even pass by without apparent concern, as the priest and Levite had. Instead he got down from his donkey, gave the beaten Jew first aid, and then helped him on the donkey and took him to a tavern and engaged a room for him, for which he paid. And he told the tavernkeeper to let the Jew stay there until he was able to travel again, and when he himself came by on his next trip he would pay any additional charges the Jew had run up.

" 'So Jesus was not only saying that we should be good to our friends, help our own class, but he was saying also that we should help our enemy, help the fellow of another race, another religion, another way of thinking.

" 'And that's why Dr. Schweitzer read the parable of the Good Samaritan tonight. That parable of Jesus is a dramatic exposition of Dr. Schweitzer's own philosophy; it's perfectly in keeping with his reverence for life, not only for the lives of members of your family or yourself or your friend, or even of your nation or your religion or your race, but also for the lives of everyone—the Negro, the Japanese, everybody, all colors, all races, all religions, all nationalities. Even your enemy has reverence for his life, if not for yours, and you must help him.' "

But Gaine Cannon suggests a more striking parallel that presents the teaching of Jesus effectively to Balsam Grove citizens and white Americans generally of this generation.

"As Jesus would be talking to us today, I think, he might tell the story like this: A prosperous white man had been beaten and robbed and left beside the highway by his assailants. In a few minutes a white man came along in his Cadillac; he saw the man lying on the shoulder of the road, but he was in a great hurry to fill a business appointment of tremendous importance. If he stopped, that would make him late for the appointment, and he might get involved with the police as a witness and have to go to court and testify, and the whole thing would be a great bother. And somebody would be along anyway in a minute or two to see to the fellow. So he sped on to his appointment.

"Pretty soon another white man in a convertible came from the other direction. He, too, spotted the man in the edge of the weeds on the shoulder of the road. But he was on his way to see his girl friend and he was about to be late. If he stopped to see about this fellow, probably just a drunk anyway, he'd likely get his clothes mussed up and the car seat soiled. The state highway patrol would be along in a few minutes and take care of the man, or maybe some poor fellow in a rattle-trap car that'll be no worse for having a dirty drunk riding in it.

"Well, the poor fellow in the rattletrap did come along. And he was a Negro. He'd been cuffed around by a white employer and he had no particular reason to put himself out to help a white man. But he stopped, and he gave the injured man first aid, and he helped him into his run-down automobile and carried him to the hospital in the city, ten miles down the road.

"Or," Dr. Cannon adds, "you might change it around and have a Negro beaten up and robbed and two Negroes come along, but do nothing for him, and then finally a poor white man rescues him. But any way you tell it—and I believe the version Jesus gave is the most dramatic and effective in putting across his teaching—this story of the Good Samaritan is a story of reverence for life. It is a story directed to every man, woman, and child; it is universal; it is the essence of the teaching of Jesus.

"The world is full of trouble, pain, hope, aspiration, death, life, frustration, inspiration. Everywhere about us a grim fight goes on, a fight for life. Billions of creatures struggle to live and not to die. On all sides we see, if we are willing to look, a tremendous reverence for living, an insatiable hunger for life. So I believe that all the highest creatures of the Creator's fashioning—all men, regardless of race or color, nationality, religion, economic status—should do everything they can to inspire and assist all other life, particularly human life, to live and enjoy the life it has been given.

"And I don't know of any place in the world," Gaine Cannon adds, "I'd rather be than right here in the mountains, among my own folk of Balsam Grove, where I can help people who really need and deserve help and who but for me might not get it."

Gaine Cannon's greatest thrill at Lambaréné was his personal interview with Dr. Schweitzer. Even telling about it is an enjoyable experience for him.

"Dr. Schweitzer met with each member of our group for at least an hour, and I was the first one called in," he says. "I don't know whether he called us in alphabetical order, or because I was the only M.D. in the group, or if there was any particular reason. At any rate, we talked for more than an hour, and though he had his interpreter there, we seldom required her help. He talked in German, but I was able to understand him very well and he understood my English. Very quickly we seemed to establish a mutual warmth of understanding and appreciation; he addressed me with the familiar *du* of the German.

"Dr. Schweitzer's little workroom is as unpretentious as the man himself. When I walked in he was sitting at his desk, which was actually only a crude table made of undressed lumber, cluttered with papers, books, bottles, and his pet cat, which stood at his left elbow and watched him write. He was seated on a flat, square stool made of the same sort of material as the table; it had no padding whatsoever, and was backless.

"He turned around to greet me and pointed to a stool like the one he was sitting on. It had been drawn right up against his. Well, I thought I would be polite and pull it back a little way so that I wouldn't be all but sitting on his lap. But he pulled it back close to him. '*Sitzen Sie hier*. Sit here,' he said. I sat down. He took my hand and held it perhaps for twenty minutes while we talked. He asked questions about Balsam Grove and the hospital, the people of our community and of the mountains generally. As he was questioning me, he got up and went over to his bookshelf, where he pulled down a geography book, and thumbing through it until he reached a map of the United States, put his stubby finger on North Carolina. *'Balsam Grove,'* he said, *'wo ist Balsam Grove?'*

" 'Here it is,' I replied, pointing to the place on the map after I had located Asheville for him. 'Balsam Grove is about here, even if it isn't marked.'

"He took his pencil, and putting the point to his lips to wet it, carefully made a dot on the map at the place I indicated. He continued to question me, about my children, about David, my eldest son, and his plans, about my helpers at the hospital. He showed what I considered an amazing knowledge of the Balsam Grove community, the hospital, and me, and I wondered where he had got the information that enabled him to ask me such searching questions. Then I discovered that he had accumulated a large folder on Balsam Grove and me that he had evidently read and remembered in considerable detail. The folder was filled with clippings and other material sent him by friends in the United States. He had not referred to the folder, however, in talking with me; he had read the material, perhaps when he received it, and now he was recalling what he had read about me and was using that to obtain further details about our work."

The group from the United States had several meetings with Dr. Schweitzer. One evening he agreed to let each person ask him a question that he would try to answer. The visitors might ask him about his philosophy, his religion, or anything else that might be puzzling them, he said. When it came Gaine Cannon's turn to question him, Dr. Cannon asked him, "Is it reasonable to believe that God does not exist outside the universe, but rather in the hearts of men?"

"Some of the people in the group shook their heads at me," Gaine Cannon recalls. " 'He won't answer that,' they whispered. 'He may just close up like a clam and walk out.' But he didn't walk out, although he pondered the question a long time before he replied.

" 'Yes, I think that's true,' he said. 'I'd hate to think that God is off somewhere, sitting on a throne and directing affairs in the world, that He is responsible for what is happening. I'd hate to believe that He directed man in the making of the atomic bomb. But if He is living and dwelling in the hearts of men and men refuse to allow Him to express Himself, then man and not God is responsible for the atomic bomb and all other evils.' "

Dr. Schweitzer, Dr. Cannon emphasizes, has written and spoken at considerable length against the atomic bomb, and the bomb is indeed one of his abominations. Dr. Phillips told Dr. Cannon that he had filled some teeth for Dr. Schweitzer on a previous meeting with him. Knowing the doctor's feeling about the bomb, said Dr. Phillips, as he was finishing the dental work on his famous patient he assured him there would be no "fallout here."

"Listen," Dr. Schweitzer had said sternly, "don't make a joke; that's a serious matter."

Dr. Schweitzer revealed to Dr. Cannon how he came to designate his philosophy as "reverence for life."

He said that one day he was going up the Ogowe River to see a missionary's wife who was ill. For days he had been trying to think of a term that would describe his philosophy. As his dugout moved up the stream, past fish jumping and hippopotami playing, suddenly an idea came to him. He was passing two small islands at the moment.

" 'What you want,' this inner voice said to me," Dr.

Schweitzer recalled for Dr. Cannon, " 'is reverence for life.' And there it was. I had the term I was seeking."

"And it is perfectly descriptive, too," Gaine Cannon says. "Before we had anything like religion, we had something in man that made him want to live, otherwise man wouldn't have continued to exist through the centuries, thousands, or millions of years, however long it has been since he arrived on earth. We call this desire to live, this determination, 'a will to live.' When you think about it, that is actually all we have, a will to live. We don't know why we are here, we don't know where we came from, we don't know where we are going. But we do have a will to live, and we know that each of us is a will to live existing among many other wills to live. So if any of us has more than another, we must share it with him, we must help him in his will to live. That desire to help him becomes what I know as reverence for life."

CHAPTER

17

THE American group of which Dr. Cannon was a member returned to New York in time to attend a dinner on January 14 given by Schweitzer enthusiasts in celebration of his birthday anniversary. Two days later Gaine Cannon was back in Balsam Grove with an increased devotion and dedication to Albert Schweitzer and his philosophy. He brought back from Lambaréné and a meeting with the *grand docteur* a new enthusiasm for translating into action and accomplishment his own version of reverence for life, which in essence paralleled that of the man he venerated.

With renewed eagerness and energy he resumed the task of completing construction of the hospital building. The exterior work on the central section and one wing had been finished; only the foundations had been dug and cinder-block walls erected to a height of three or four feet on the other wing. As fast as he could collect money that did not have to be allotted for drugs and medicines and other expenses of his clinic, he spent it for materials, and he solicited free labor and paid out of his own funds wages of skilled laborers adept at setting stones. And patients continued to bring in rounded river rocks that quickly went into the rising walls.

Gaine Cannon conceived and put into operation ingenious schemes for adding funds to the hospital treasury. A large manufacturing firm in South Carolina provided barrels of candy at very reasonable cost, and the candy was sold, again reasonably, to visitors, some of whom drove many miles to buy it, sometimes fifteen or twenty pounds at a time. The profit went into the hospital fund. Other items were also put on sale, including mountain handicraft products, jams and jellies, and items of many other kinds, and the money earned from them was added to the growing account.

An innovation of Gaine Cannon's that has done much more than simply add dollars to the hospital building program was the establishment of Hospital Day. Dr. Cannon explains:

"We decided to set aside one day each summer as Albert Schweitzer Memorial Hospital Day, and we selected the second Sunday in August. It has grown into an event that our folk look forward to from one year to another. On this day they congregate in our little cove from many miles around. Balsam Grove people who have moved away, some to distant communities, try to get back home for the day, and as a result it has become an important home-coming occasion for the entire region as well as a great event for the hospital and its supporters."

Each year during the two or three weeks preceding Hospital Day it is widely advertised in the papers and on the radio, and invariably a large assemblage is present by the time the picnic dinner is spread on tables set up on the hospital grounds.

"We always try to get a good speaker, a Congressman or some other person well known in our section, and to supplement the speaking we have much music, singing, and playing by musicians popular in our mountain region. But the big event is the picnic dinner itself, and the opportunity it gives friends to visit and talk, many of them for the first time since Hospital Day the previous year."

One Sunday there were some fifteen hundred persons at the festivities, and in the mountains that is a tremendous outpouring. That day, as on other Hospital Days, the picnic tables stretched a hundred feet and on them were country ham, chicken, roast beef, roast pork, mutton, bear, venison, goat, pies by the scores, cakes, jams and jellies, tomatoes, sandwiches, food of every description, and great quantities of it.

On each Hospital Day, too, a collection is taken for the hospital. Outsiders express amazement at the amount of money given. At Hospital Day in August of 1962, bad weather on the previous several days had cut down the attendance and perhaps hardly more than four hundred people, including children and even babies, were present. But when hats were passed through the crowd and the money contributed was counted, it was disclosed that more than seventeen hundred dollars had been given, almost all of it by people of the community.

"That represents a very generous gift by the citizens of Balsam Grove," Dr. Cannon points out. "A dollar or two in a great many cases would be a large gift, and one that represents a sacrifice. But our folk love their hospital; they are proud of it, and they do all they can to promote and support it. And their enthusiasm for it makes me all the more determined to see it through to completion and successful operation."

The last Hospital Day—the second Sunday in August 1963 —was also a successful venture that brought a large assemblage of Balsam Grove people into the little cove to enjoy a bountiful picnic dinner, tramp through the almost-completed hospital structure and contribute more dollars into the fund that is insuring its construction.

Each second Sunday in August brings not only Balsam Grove folk into the little cove through which twisting Shoal Creek murmurs its way, but also one or more notables from the world outside, occasionally from long distances. Visitors to Balsam Grove, some of them on Hospital Day, have included even Dr. Schweitzer's daughter, Mrs. Rhena Eckart, and her husband, who in the summer of 1962 spent several days there. It was Mrs. Eckart's first visit. She had been to the United States, but had never been South before. She was making a tour of the various Schweitzer institutions, she reported to Dr. Cannon. She had come first to New York, to the Albert Schweitzer Fellowship, and then to Balsam Grove, from which, she told Dr. Cannon, she and Mr. Eckart would go on a visit to L'Hôpital Albert Schweitzer in Haiti. She reported that she was also planning to visit other Schweitzer institutions, including a hospital in one of the South American countries administered by a German friend of the Schweitzer family.

Another warmly welcomed guest was Dr. Marion Mill Preminger, whom Dr. Cannon had met during his visit to Lambaréné. Dr. Preminger was accompanied by her husband, Dr. Albert Meyer, a noted New York architect and builder. She had just returned to the United States from her tenth trip to Lambaréné.

That was not her first visit to Balsam Grove, however; she had come down the year before.

Dr. Preminger brought a gift for the hospital, a large oil painting of the hospital compound at Lambaréné. It was one of the most appreciated and highly valued of all the gifts received at the 1962 Hospital Day exercises.

"Dr. Preminger told me that the painting had quite a history," Gaine Cannon says. "She said that it had traveled at least fifty thousand miles on lecture trips she has made and that the Academy of Medicine in New York or Washington was supposed to have got it, but that she decided instead to give it to us. We are very proud to have it. We have packed it carefully and put it away in a locked room for the present, but when the hospital building is finished we are going to frame it and hang it in a prominent position in the lobby alongside a big picture of Dr. Schweitzer himself."

Within a year and a half after Gaine Cannon's return to Balsam Grove the walls of the hospital were nearing completion, including the stone outer course; the roof was on, and the outside of the structure was virtually finished. There remained the task of pouring floors in the last wing to be constructed and the finishing of the interior. Dr. Cannon looked to the summer of 1964 as the date for beginning operation of the hospital; perhaps dedication of the plant would be the main event of the Hospital Day program. Meanwhile he was making plans for equipping and furnishing it.

"We've already bought the furniture for it from a hospital in Charlotte, North Carolina, that was refurnishing its institution. We were most fortunate in being able to purchase this furniture, which is of good quality and appearance and will serve us most acceptably. And by purchasing it we are able to furnish each patient's room completely, I think, with the exception of the mattress, for ninety-seven dollars. Ordinarily we'd have to pay from five hundred to six hundred dollars for this. The equipment includes bed, dresser, bedside table, overbed table, and chairs.

"As we open the hospital, it will be a thirty-bed institution. That is in addition to beds in the delivery room, the recovery room, and a few other places."

In planning the hospital Dr. Cannon made provision for three or four small wards—the number depends upon how certain interior partitions are set—each with three or four beds in it. "We don't intend to have large wards," he says. "Large wards tend to make the patient uncomfortable; he is crowded into a place where some may be quite sick and others not very ill. So we'll have small wards, and only three or four of them, certainly at the beginning."

But as he completes plans for the opening, Dr. Cannon already foresees the early necessity of adding to the structure. "With the enlargement of the services our clinic has been able to provide through the expansion of facilities made possible in the opening of the hospital, I am confident we'll see a large increase in the number of patients coming to Balsam Grove, particularly from other communities." He predicts patients will be coming from South Carolina, and not only the Pickens community, where he formerly practiced and operated the hospital he built there, but also from Greenville, Anderson, and Oconee counties. And others, he thinks, will be coming from beyond Asheville, in North Carolina.

"When I came up here from Pickens, I had 26,000 records on patients, individual cards of patients I had seen while I was operating the hospital there. Those are patients," he emphasizes, "not cases—26,000 different persons. So my patients down there were coming from other counties also, and many of these patients followed me when I came up here. We expect them to continue to come, as well as others from places a considerable distance from Balsam Grove."

Fortunately, in drawing his plans Gaine Cannon provided for a projected expansion that would add architectural value as well as physical accommodations. "I planned the structure so that we can go back with a third wing from the central section," he reveals. "It will require some excavating into the side of the slope behind the building, but that can be done with little difficulty. And in another few years, maybe before then, we may have to make that addition, because the work in the community is growing rapidly and with new people coming into this community—not counting patients we expect from other communities—need for expanded medical service and hospital care is bound to develop rapidly."

In recent years Dr. Cannon has been nurturing a fond hope.

"But I'm afraid it is a hope that will never materialize," he says. "I had hoped that we might be able to get Dr. Schweitzer down to Balsam Grove for the opening of the hospital. I'd had all sorts of daydreams about it. We'd have the Governor of North Carolina over for the dedication ceremonies—we hope to have him anyway—and perhaps even the President. But the marvelous thing would be that Albert Schweitzer would be here for the dedication of our little hospital named for him.

"I have asked him to come. I told him how much we wanted him, how tremendously honored we'd be to have him in North Carolina, in America. I asked him when I was over at Lambaréné. But he only shook his head. 'I'd like very much to go,' he said, '*aber Ich bin zu alt*. I'm too old.' And I know that is true. It would be a long and hard journey for him. But if we could get him, wouldn't it really be tremendous!"

Although Dr. Cannon has a good start toward furnishing his hospital, he still must arrange for the installation of such required equipment, for example, as an X-ray machine and laboratory apparatus.

"Of course, we realized a decade ago, when our dreams of establishing an institution here in our cove were beginning to take shape, that our little Balsam Grove community alone wouldn't be able to build or support even a small hospital. So in drawing up our plans we have always contemplated the hospital's serving outlying communities, and now there are areas of three counties reached by its services. The hospital consequently has become the center, the focal point, of this enlarged community.

"So we have been giving much thought to a plan—and we have done some actual preliminary work toward implementing it—for the development of what we shall probably call the Albert Schweitzer Community, which will be comparable to shopping centers springing up so rapidly in suburban areas of our cities. We plan the establishment of this shopping and service center at Balsam Grove in a small, level valley beside the highway where the lane from the hospital enters it, and we are virtually certain we'll have it built, in part, at any rate, within the next year.

"Such a center is greatly needed in the Balsam Grove area, and we are confident that it can be operated profitably. We foresee the building there of an old-fashioned country store where all kinds of products would be on sale. We would build it, too, like an old-time general merchandising store, with a porch across the front and benches where the folk could sit down awhile and exchange the news, and maybe play a game of checkers on a warm summer afternoon. And of course we would have a barbershop and a beauty parlor, a service station and garage where cars could be repaired, a washerette, and perhaps other services. We would have a section set aside for recreation, too, on which we would have a baseball diamond, perhaps a miniature golf layout, maybe a small bowling alley, later on somewhere nearby a nine-hole golf course.

"In the store—or we might have a separate building for it —we would have a market where our folk could sell products they have grown or made, country hams, sausage, liver mush, jams and preserves and jellies, string beans, corn, okra, tomatoes, potatoes, cabbage, honey, homemade sorghum molasses, and items of their handicraft, woven rugs, carved things, pottery—there's no end to what might be handled in our little shopping community.

"Think of the revenue it would bring in by thus giving our people an opportunity to earn money in a region where the average income is very low and at the same time providing services they cannot now obtain without driving long distances into Brevard or some other town. And it would help keep our money in our community."

But the establishment of this shopping and service center at Balsam Grove is only a part of the doctor's program for the development of the community and the further financial buttressing of the hospital.

"In connection with this Schweitzer Community we would have also some small industries that would give additional employment to our folk around Balsam Grove. Right now we are planning—and the plans are well under way already—to put up a small plant for producing homogenized peanut butter, salted peanuts, peanut crackers and peanut sandwiches, and perhaps peanut candy. We are going to house this operation in a large structure I have been building on top of the hill across in front of the hospital, which was originally planned as a lodge where we would accommodate visitors. Our next project, according to present planning, is to erect on the excavation site of an old swimming pool behind what was the farmhouse a little plant where we'll make products for babies, such as baby oil, baby powder, detergents. We will use the pool as the basement and build a story above it. After creating the pool several years ago, we realized it was a hazard, because we

[209]

did not have and could not afford to employ enough personnel to stay on duty about the pool and there was always the possibility that a child might drown. So we abandoned the pool before we had completed it, and now we are going to turn it into something that will be useful and will provide profitable employment for perhaps a half dozen of our Balsam Grove folk."

Dr. Cannon has arranged for a large manufacturing firm in South Carolina to sell Balsam Grove products to the firm's market. Another company, which manufactures candy products, will handle the sales of the peanut products.

"These products will be labeled and sold under the name of the Albert Schweitzer Memorial Hospital," Dr. Cannon reveals. "We have received Dr. Schweitzer's permission to use his name, since these businesses will not be ordinary commercial enterprises but operations sponsored by the hospital, with all profits from their operations going to the hospital. This will be true of the other enterprises down in the Albert Schweitzer Community also; the profit from the general store, the barbershop, the beauty parlor, all of it, will go to the hospital, and ultimately, of course, to the people whom the hospital will be serving."

This is the way Dr. Cannon proposes to pass on the profits of these various commercial ventures to the hospital and through it to the patients:

"We will set up an agency to lend money to patients with which they will pay their hospital and doctor bills, and the lending agency will pay the hospital. We will make the terms to suit the patient, maybe fifty cents a week, maybe a dollar or so, maybe nothing in the case of a patient who is unable to pay. In that way we will keep the hospital out of the red, because it will get its money whether the patient can pay or not.

The lending agency will be holding the bag. It will help our folk who can't pay to keep their self-respect; it will keep them from being pauperized by making them know that they do owe a bill whether they can pay it or not. They won't feel that they can just come in any time they wish free of charge, as is now the case with a few of them. We shall charge probably two or three per cent interest on the money owed, and that will help take care of the amount owed but never collected. But the principal support of the agency to the hospital other than that afforded through the repayment of funds borrowed by patients will be the money coming from profits earned in the operation of the Albert Schweitzer Community enterprises, including the peanut products and baby toilet and care supplies.

"With funds thus made available the hospital will be able to provide more efficient service. For instance, one of the long-time needs here has been a surgeon. I am a general practitioner, and though I do minor surgery quite frequently, I am not trained to do general surgery, and I wouldn't attempt it. I am busy as it is with my general practice; in fact, I am going day and night and then can hardly stay abreast of my work. But when we get the hospital in operation, we expect to have a surgeon. In addition we may get a young surgeon starting his career who will be glad to come to our little hospital and work under the supervision of an experienced one, and that would give us two surgeons here and a surgery service, in emergencies, around the clock; that would be of especial efficacy in a mountain region such as ours.

"We are confident that we will have little trouble staffing our hospital with good men. There are always capable men retiring, surgeons, X-ray technicians, internal medicine specialists, and doctors in other fields who don't want to sit down and completely quit, who want to keep their hands in, so to speak. We feel that we may be able to get several such men to locate here. After all, we're in a mountain resort area and because of our climate and scenery should attract good men who would be able to help us tremendously. And with our lending agency operating we could see to it that these specialists were paid for their services. If the patient couldn't pay, the lending agency would.

"Suppose we should need a specialist from one of the medical centers, say Charlotte or Winston-Salem or Chapel Hill or Duke, to operate on a charity patient. We could bring him up here or send the patient to him, and he would get his money. He would know that it was a charity patient and would make his charge on that basis, we would hope and expect, but he would receive some money for his services whether the patient was able to pay or not."

Dr. Cannon is confident, too, that the hospital will have no trouble in keeping adequate nursing personnel. He was further encouraged because of his success in obtaining the State Department's approval for a young woman he met during his visit to Lambaréné to come to the United States. She is Fraulein Gertrud Raschke, a native of the Königsberg region of Germany and a devoted adherent of Dr. Schweitzer's, who came to Balsam Grove in the spring of 1963 after having spent more than two years working with him in Africa. She plans to remain at Balsam Grove and become an American citizen.

Another advantage in having an agency to lend money for the payment of doctor and hospital bills, Dr. Cannon points out, will be the ability of any patient to gain immediate admission to the Albert Schweitzer Memorial Hospital, or if it should be required for special examination or treatment, to any other hospital.

"We are always hearing of seriously ill patients being kept waiting in hospital lobbies while their families seek frantically to get up money to pay for their admissions. Some of the stories are exaggerated, but it is a fact that quite often patients very ill lose several hours of vital treatment while efforts are being made to locate funds. The patient may be waiting in pain while someone tries to come up with fifty or a hundred dollars.

"In our hospital the patient, whether he has a million dollars or a dime, will be admitted immediately and his treatment begun. All he has to do—or have someone do for him—is to sign a simple lending agency agreement."

But even so Dr. Cannon is invariably asked when he tells of his plans for the lending agency, could the hospital avoid having to suspend operations because of unpaid bills of patients who could not or would not pay the agency?

"If they simply refused to pay even though they were able, the agency could legally collect," he replies, "but if they were unable to pay, it would lose the money lent the patient. We have honest folk in our mountains; they pay their debts, and few incur debts when they know that they won't be able to repay them. So we feel that our losses from those who don't pay will be comparatively small. The losses from patients unable to pay their bills will be marked off as charity. But there will be this very important difference in our hospital's charitable operations and those of other such institutions. Our hospital won't be paying the charity bill. The lending agency will pay it. And we feel sure that the profits from our commercial operations at Balsam Grove will more than offset these losses, and even enable us to expand our services and in all probability enlarge our physical facilities."

Gaine Cannon has already begun to envision the expansion

of the services of his hospital, not yet in operation, into communities more isolated than Balsam Grove. Tentatively, he reveals, he is hoping to start clinics at Tuckaseigee, a small place across the mountains, and several other such settlements, where a doctor on his staff would spend an afternoon or two a week.

"We'd rent a house, or maybe take over an old schoolhouse that had been abandoned with the consolidation of schools, and equip it as a clinic. That is what they want us to do, for instance, in one of the communities I have been visiting over in Jackson County. They want us to come two days a week. They promise they will provide a building, fix it up for us the way we want it, and keep it up; we would furnish our own equipment, drugs, and supplies.

"We might start one also in Cashiers, another place up here, and another at High Hampton, where there is no doctor, even though it is a noted summer resort frequented by wealthy people who have been going there for years. In fact, there isn't a doctor living within miles of High Hampton, and when someone gets sick there, especially if it's in the middle of the night, it's often a long time before medical help can be obtained or the sick person can be brought to the doctor."

Dr. Cannon envisions other medical services for his region after the hospital is in operation. "We might even be able to establish a modest nursing service that could be of tremendous help to our folk; through our clinic we might get a co-operative program with the health authorities under way that would enable us to provide pre-school preventive inoculations and vaccinations, thereby saving many parents from having to make the forty-mile drive, there and back, to Brevard or some other place even farther away. We could encourage that work as well as other programs in preventive medicine and public health."

In all probability, too, Dr. Cannon is confident, his hospital could arrange for the public health people in Brevard to cooperate with his community clinics by sending out nurses to assist in providing these pre-school inoculations and vaccinations and to aid in the promotion of other health programs, including the examinations of eyes and throats of children and adults to see if glasses should be fitted and tonsilectomies are required or other physical needs can be given proper attention.

"We might be able even to provide such service through our clinics in these various communities without going into the red," Dr. Cannon forecasts, "but if we can't we will have our Albert Schweitzer Community profits to make up the difference between the red and the black. And after all, our purpose will not be to make money but to provide greatly needed health services. With a little push from everybody this program, which now is only a hope, a dream unrealized, could quickly snowball into something of tremendous significance to this whole mountain region."

Happily, Dr. Cannon foresaw from the beginning of his dream for a little hospital in the cove through which Shoal Creek runs that it would have to have, if it was to be effectively administered, a broader supporting base than the little community of Balsam Grove with its some seventy families, none wealthy and many extremely poor.

"So we set up the hospital under a board of trustees, and these trustees, seven in all, were selected from a fairly large section. One of them is from over in Jackson County. The hospital is incorporated. It owns itself. We decided not to make it community-owned because that would limit its operations and services from the start, and anyway, our little immediate community of Balsam Grove couldn't support it. I am one of the trustees, and so far as I know, this is the only hospital, certainly the only one in this part of the country, that has a doctor on its board. Other hospitals won't have them; I suppose they think that doctors aren't good businessmen. They may have a doctor or two sit in on their board meetings, but as a general thing, they won't have one on their boards."

But Gaine Cannon, even though he is a doctor, has been able to give the hospital board a good deal of sound advice because of the experience he has gained in building three clinics and two other hospitals. In drawing the plans for the hospital structure, in fact, he even saved them the cost of an architect.

CHAPTER
18

THE automobile, rattling across the little wooden bridge, awakened him. An early patient probably coming by on his way to work over in town, or someone bringing a piece of equipment or supplies for the hospital, Gaine Cannon thought.

He threw back the light covering, swung his feet around to the floor, and stood up ponderously. He hunched his shoulders forward and back, swung his arms rapidly to cross each other, forearms parallel with the floor, over his chest, and twisted to one side and then the other to smooth the night kinks from his stiff, aching back. Then he quickly put his clothes on; buttoning his plaid short-sleeved shirt, he opened the front door of the Albert Schweitzer Museum and walked out on the dew-wet grass terrace.

Lately Dr. Cannon had been sleeping in this room, which he had added as the bottom of a U formed by it in joining his apartment with one of similar size and shape some thirty feet away. Into this new, long, stone-walled chamber, with its backside built into the steep hill rising precipitously from the flat of the cove, he had assembled his various Schweitzer me-

[217]

mentos: books and pamphlets by and about the *grand docteur*, letters from him or relating to him, busts in wood and bronze of Dr. Schweitzer, pictures of him and his hospital at Lambaréné, the odds and ends of more than three decades of collecting everything he could that was in any way concerned with Albert Schweitzer.

Dr. Cannon had placed in one corner a pine single bed made by a carpenter in Balsam Grove. A shelf at the head of the bed held a lamp and books, medical journals, and articles he might want to read before going to sleep, and the shelf was further burdened with an accumulation of Schweitzer oddments. Gaine Cannon told friends who commented on it that he had moved into the museum to sleep because he had discovered that he could rest better there. In his regular bed on the gallery overlooking the living room of his apartment he was close to the sloping roof, and sleeping up there, he seemed to experience a feeling of stuffiness, so that he awakened in the mornings little refreshed. Perhaps, he agreed, it was his tendency to claustrophobia that caused this feeling when he slept in his gallery bed. But he knew that soon now, before he could open the museum to visitors, next year in 1964, he would have to find some other place for his bed.

Standing on the terrace in the cool freshness of early morning, Gaine Cannon began to come alive to the stirrings of the new day. In the apple tree overhanging the creek a raucous jay and a pair of mockingbirds chattered and quarreled, and in the distance beyond the high hill in front of him a coon hound bayed. Fifty paces below and ahead, Shoal Creek rippled serenely over the rounded stones. To his left rose and yellow slim fingers of light stiffened upward from the sun, which in another two hours would show itself above the rim of heavily forested hills hemming in the cove, but which now

[218]

sent long purpled shadows westward past the winding channel of the cheek and the bridge to engulf even the little hospital, proud in acid-scrubbed stone walls and freshly painted door and window frames and almost ready for its first influx of patients.

Today would be another warm one, Gaine Cannon's bones told him, but he would not complain if the temperature went past ninety, he had promised. Six months ago had he stood here long, he would have frozen; never in his memory had he experienced a colder winter in these mountains. On a day in January, he remembered as he stood here in short-sleeved shirt, from atop Mount Pisgah, fifteen miles behind him to the north as the freezing winds would blow into this cove, the reading had been twenty-four degrees below zero. The heavy snows, the ice and sleet, the hazardous highways and the steep, twisting, narrow trails up to hidden-away cabins and all but obliterated by the deepening snow, and the bone-chilling cold had made his work harder and more dangerous than it had ever been before. The returning warm weather had brought not only respite from his rheumatism but a restored peace of mind. Even with the weather again severely cold during the coming winter, he reasoned, he would not have to visit so many almost inaccessible mountain homes since the hospital would be in operation. The patients could be brought to the hospital and kept there until they had recovered.

And it would not be long until the Albert Schweitzer Memorial Hospital would be in routine operation, he was confident. Surely by late fall they would be able to show the visiting throng through a modern hospital, well equipped, efficiently administered, and already dismissing patients cured of a multiplicity of ailments. Then, he told himself, he would be spending the greater part of his time in the hospital rather than in his little Renault, fighting his way to and from cabin homes lost deep in coves or perched precariously on steep hillsides. Then he would be able to provide more efficient medical service to many more of his beloved hill folk.

But he turned quickly from contemplating the newly finished structure and what it soon would accomplish. Down at the parking space beside the farmhouse-clinic—which soon would be no longer the clinic but probably a guest house for members of patients' families or other overnight visitors— stood a battered automobile. He had seen it before, he knew, but he did not immediately recognize it. Very likely the driver had gone into Hugh's little house, nearby. But in that instant Hugh came out the front door of the clinic and started toward the doctor.

"RFL, Doc!" he shouted, and threw up his hands as he saw Gaine Cannon on the terrace above the cove. The initials of "reverence for life" have become a familiar greeting among members of Gaine Cannon's staff.

"RFL, Hugh. Nice morning."

"Yeh, Doc, but it's agoin' to be a hot'n."

"I don't mind that. Who came up in that car? A patient, or somebody bringing something for the hospital?"

"Neither one, Doc." Hugh had reached the foot of the terrace. "One o' old man Coley's boys. Come to tell you his daddy's awantin' you to come."

"Another heart attack?"

"That's what he said, Doc. Said it was mighty bad, and the old man's acallin' for you to come quick as you can."

"What'd he do to bring it on? Did the boy say, Hugh?"

"Said his old man got up early and was aworkin' his garden with a hoe."

"I thought so. If the old goat would just do what I tell

him—" But quickly the doctor's scowl was gone and his round face lighted. "You can't blame him, though; I doubt if anybody could convince me to lie around and do nothing." His expression was serious again. "Hugh, if we just had the hospital open, we could keep him here awhile and maybe he'd make it. But this way—" He shook his head. "But run down there and tell the boy that he can tell his daddy we'll be over right away. And, Hugh, get my bag and put it in the Renault. We'd better not wait for Helen. Old man Coley's likely in bad shape. And don't forget to put that oxygen tank in!"